10 PRINCIPLES OF
GOOD ADVERTISING

I WANT YOUR

MONEY, JEWELRY, CAR, BOAT AND HOUSE.

Thanks to civil asset forfeiture laws, possessions that took you a lifetime to acquire can be taken in the blink of an eye, or more accurately, the flash of a badge. Probable cause. That's all police are required to show before they can seize everything from family photos to your life savings. The forfeiture laws were designed as a new government weapon in the "war on drugs." But they've done little more than provide law enforcement with a license to steal. After all, who can you call when the police are the ones robbing you? Help us defend your rights. Support the ACLU. To learn more, visit www.aclu.org/forfeiture.

10 ADVERTISING PRINCIPLES

ROBERT SHORE

VIVAYS PUBLISHING

Published by Vivays Publishing Ltd
www.vivays-publishing.com

A catalogue record for this book is
available from the British Library
ISBN 978-1-908126-30-6

Publishing Director: Lee Ripley

Design: Draught Associates

Cover and frontispiece: Courtesy of
The Advertising Archives

Printed in China

CONTENTS

INTRODUCTION

INTRODUCTION

Advertising is arguably the world's most powerful industry. It not only helps manufacturers to sell billions of pounds' worth of goods, it also plays an important role in drawing attention to social issues – think of the way advertising has been used to alter attitudes to smoking – and can even influence who will form the next government. When Bill Bernbach, the architect of the so-called 1960s 'Creative Revolution', died, *Harper's Bazaar* said he had 'probably had a greater impact on American culture than any of the distinguished writers and artists who have appeared in [our] pages'. That was written in the early 1980s, when advertising seemed to have moved to centre stage of Western culture. Even so, given the historic power of the industry and Bernbach's particular part in remodelling it, it was hardly an exaggeration.

Advertising is used not only to
sell products for manufacturers
but also to win elections for
political parties. Top: BMW, 2004.
Above: The Conservative Party, 1979

Attitudes to smoking have
been radically affected by bold
government-sponsored health-
awareness campaigns. California
Department of Health Services, 2000s

A brief history

The origins of advertising can be traced back at least as far
as ancient Egypt. Advertising forms that are still popular
today such as posters and illustrated newspaper ads first
appeared in the late eighteenth century, at the onset of
modern consumer society. A further leap came at the end of
the nineteenth century, with the emergence of mass branded
goods and the corresponding need for rival companies to
promote the particular virtues of essentially similar products,
persuading customers to buy their variety of, say, breakfast
cereal rather than a competing maker's. The first specialist
advertising agencies emerged around the same time to
negotiate between newspapers and magazines with ad space
to sell and manufacturers with products to promote; the hub
of this inchoate industry developed on New York's Madison
Avenue, which to this day remains one of the major creative
centres in what has since become an increasingly
globalised business.

lung, Bob.

California Department Of Health Services.
Funded By The Tobacco Tax Initiative.

© 1998 California Department of Health Services

What is advertising?

So what is advertising exactly? We all recognise it when we see it: it's those attention-grabbing collages of images and words that shout at us from billboards in the street, bookend the TV programmes we watch and cluster around the editorial content we read in print and online. A definition of the process might be: advertising is about creating a message about something (usually a product or service) and then using different media (everything from leaflets to cinema ads) to communicate that message to a target group of people in the hope that they will react in a particular way – which in all likelihood means triggering a Pavlovian reaction so that they buy or in some other way engage with that product or service. This book looks at the different elements in this definition and provides an introduction – through a discussion of 10 Principles – to the way the advertising industry works and the various processes involved in creating successful ads.

The growing media-literacy
of consumers has encouraged
advertisers to adopt more knowing
campaign strategies to make its
target audience look more closely.
French Connection, 2000s

Some people claim to be unaffected by advertising; many more are anxious about its influence. Attitudes to television advertising, for instance, have always been strongly ambivalent in the UK (much less so in the US). When Britain's first commercial channel, ITV, was launched on 22 September 1955, viewers were somewhat sniffily reassured by an announcer: 'We shall not be bothered by a violinist stopping in the middle of a solo to advise us on his favourite brand of cigarettes. Nor will Hamlet halt his soliloquy to tell us what toothpaste they are using at Elsinore.' But when it actually fell time for the first advert to be aired – for Gibbs SR toothpaste – an altogether more enthusiastic attitude was expressed: 'And now the moment you've all been waiting for – it's time for the commercial break.' In popular lore, the ad breaks represent the moment when viewers walk away from their TVs to put the kettle on, and while that certainly happens, the truth can't be quite so straightforward since these pauses in the editorial programming have regularly had a huge impact on national life – bestselling products have been launched, national catchphrases have been coined, attitudes have been definitively changed.

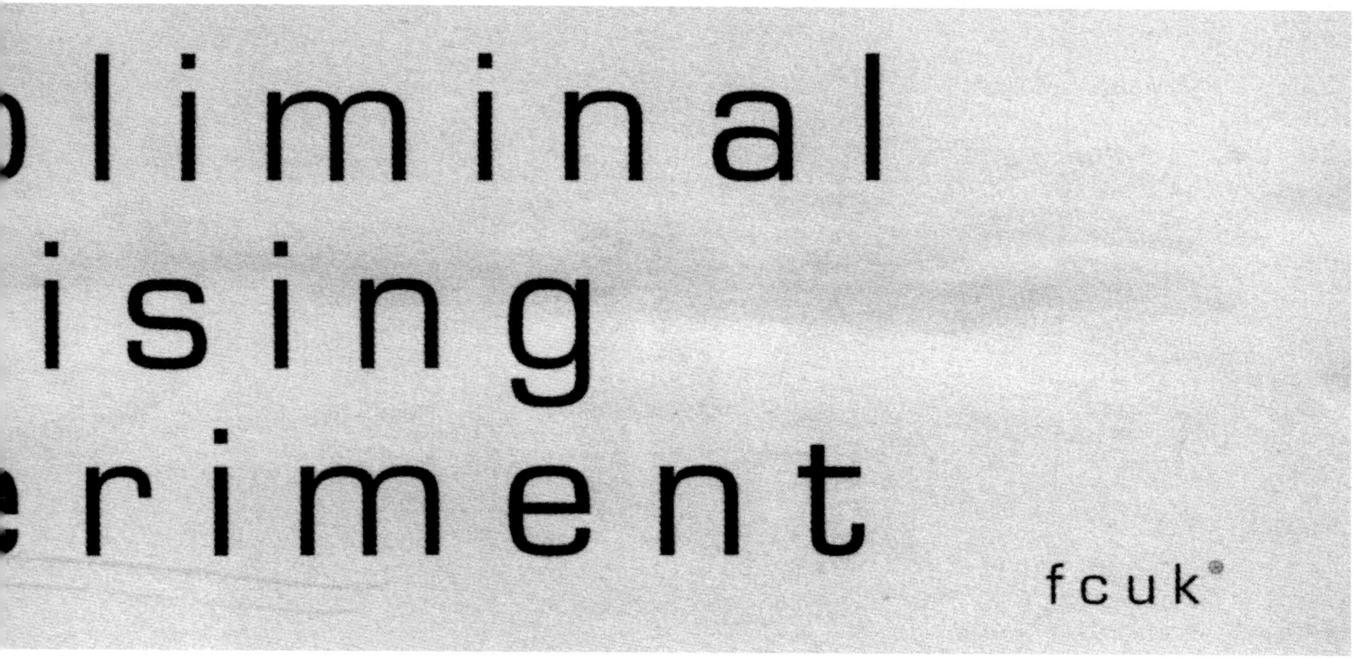

oliminal
ising
eriment
fcuk®

It seems reasonable to conclude, then, that most people quite like ads – the number of books and TV programmes entitled 'The 100 Greatest Ads' and the like is testament to that. So the threat posed to television advertising by digital television recorders (DTRs) such as TiVo and services such as Sky+, which theoretically allow viewers to fast-forward through or skip the ads in recorded programmes, has probably been exaggerated. Indeed, some early research suggested that DTR technology encourages people to watch more television in general, and that even with time-shifted viewing a significant percentage of ads are still watched at normal speed.

That shouldn't surprise us. After all, not only are ads often fun, in functional terms they're an essential part of everyday life in a market-oriented society. Advertising is there to convey the essence of a given product and what makes it different from its rivals. In theory, therefore, anyone who wants to make an informed choice when purchasing goods or services from competing providers *needs* to be aware of it.

All the same, it's never been easy to capture consumers' attention – and it's getting harder all the time. As long ago as 1759, Samuel Johnson declared that 'Advertisements are now so numerous they are very negligently perused'. Research at the end of the last century, before the explosion in internet use, variously suggested that the average person was exposed to between 150 and 3,000 commercial messages a day. Even if the truth is closer to the lower rather than the upper figure there, everyone in the developed world now comes into contact with a vast amount of advertising from an early age. As a result, consciously or otherwise, we have all become good at recognising classic advertising strategies – shock, sex, humour, fantasy – and at filtering out messages that we don't want to hear. 'You are not writing a sitcom somebody enjoys watching,' seasoned copywriter Luke Sullivan warns fellow advertising professionals in *Hey Whipple, Squeeze This*. 'You are writing something most people try to avoid.' Advertisers have consequently found themselves having to adopt increasingly outlandish 'guerrilla' strategies to circumvent audiences' defences.

Another problem that advertisers face is fragmentation. There was a time when a huge swathe of the population could be counted on to watch a particular TV programme – *The Ed Sullivan Show* in the US, perhaps, or *Coronation Street* in the UK – so if an advertiser bought a space in the ad break it could be fairly certain that its message was being delivered to a sizeable proportion of the population. 'One spot in *Coronation Street* would get you 50 per cent of the population,' says Mike Widdis, former Board Account Director at Young and Rubicam and now chairman of Rathbone Perception Media. 'Now, in London, it gets 10 per cent of that. The audience is so difficult to reach by comparison.' In addition, there's been a huge increase in the number of products on offer too. 'When Bill Bernbach started back in the 1950s, there was very little on the shelves. There are so many more *things* now,' says Widdis. Making yourself stand out from the crowd is consequently very difficult – and only getting more so.

Volkswagen recycling

Volkswagen. Wie anders?

The growing ecological consciousness
of the past few decades has had
a major impact on the way cars –
viewed as an environmental threat
themselves – are advertised.
Volkswagen, 1990s

How ads force their way into our consciousness varies wildly. Some make a beeline for the brain's central control tower, laying siege to it with infectious catchphrases and jingles until we can seemingly take no more and just agree to surrender and obey their orders, while others adopt more playfully insidious tactics to secure assent to their messages. The latter route has been pursued with greater frequency in the past few decades, with advertisers engaging in a knowing game with increasingly media-literate consumers capable of relishing the postmodern wit of an ironic or self-reflexive campaign strategy.

Creating a campaign

Most advertising campaigns are created by specialist agencies in response to briefs from clients – the generic name given to the manufacturers, corporations or other types of organisation that want to promote what they do in this way. Though some companies produce their advertising materials in-house, hiring an outside agency can bring fresh ideas and a healthy dose of objectivity to the process.

The client is always wrong?

In commerce the cliché has it that the customer is always right, but in advertising – in traditional agency lore at any rate – the client rarely is. As long ago as 1933, in *Murder Must Advertise*, Dorothy L. Sayers – who worked in advertising before becoming a novelist and is generally credited with coming up with the toucan symbol for Guinness – had her aristocratic sleuth, Lord Peter Wimsey, go to work undercover at a London ad agency named Pym's, where he was quickly informed: 'You'll soon find that the biggest obstacle to good advertising is the client.' Bill Bernbach said something similar several decades later when he announced: 'We don't permit any client to give us ground rules. Let me put it this way. We think we will never know as much about a product as a client. After all, he sleeps and breathes his product.... By the same token, we firmly believe that he can't know as much about advertising. Because we live and breathe that all day long.' For Bernbach, the advertising agency's freedom of operation was more important than securing any particular client's business, as he illustrated in the following anecdote. 'A very, very big prospect once said to me, "What would you say, Bill, if you were told exactly where to put the logo and what size it would be [on an ad]?" I had ten million dollars riding on my answer and I said, "I would say we were the wrong agency for you."' Such bullishness is regularly on display in the confrontations between clients and Sterling Cooper's creative department in Matthew Weiner's acclaimed HBO series *Mad Men*, which is set at the time of the Bernbach-led Madison Avenue 'Creative Revolution'. The reality, however, is usually less black and white. Just as good advertising agencies need to know how to sell products to consumers, they also need to know how to sell their creative ideas to clients. For their part, clients need to be open-minded: work created in a climate of fear is rarely of high quality, and work conceived to placate a client that is too fixated on having its own way is often a disaster. Great advertising is usually the result of a real partnership between agency and client, one that is founded on trust; it rarely grows out of a more adversarial relationship. Within an advertising agency, it is the account manager's job to ensure that such trust exists.

Sometimes the connection between a particular brand and its symbol – in this case a toucan – isn't immediately obvious. The ad's message is impressively clear, however. Guinness, 1930s

From client brief to creative brief

The process of creating a new advertising campaign usually begins with the 'client brief', which is presented verbally to the advertising agency by the client and provides key information about the client and its objectives. In short, the brief needs to set out what the client hopes to achieve as a result of the campaign. As with any road map, the brief needs not only to indicate the client's desired destination but also to mark its starting point: that is, it needs to assess the client's current position. A good deal of honesty is required to do this properly: carrying out a SWOT (Strengths, Weaknesses, Opportunities, Threats) analysis may help. Once the client's present position in the marketplace has been determined, it becomes possible to talk about the goals of the new advertising campaign. These might include launching a new product, increasing sales of a pre-existing product, convincing ex-users to try a particular brand again, or persuading current users to use it more often, developing brand recognition generally or altering broader perceptions of the brand. In the brief the client also needs to say something about its target audience since the campaign will need to be moulded to fit that audience.

This client brief now needs to be translated into a 'creative brief' by the advertising agency, for presentation back to the client. Traditionally, full-service agencies have five main departments, all of which will be involved in the process of creating and delivering the campaign: account managers, who liaise directly with the clients; the 'creatives', who come up with and refine the creative concept; media planners, who are responsible for deciding where the ads will appear; and the production department, who take care of all aspects of actually making the ads. The process begins, however, with the fifth department, the account planning team, conducting research into the target audience and its attitude towards the brand and the market generally. Which brings us tidily to our First Principle of Advertising.

THE LAND ROVER S1 PHONE Incredibly tough

LAND ROVER

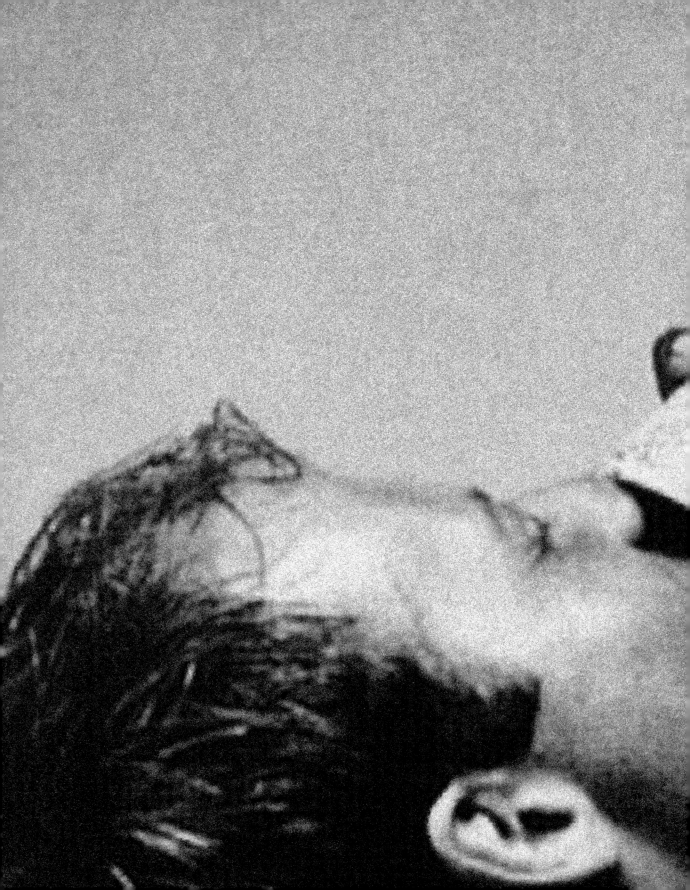

PRINCIPLE 1
KNOW YOUR AUDIENCE

PRINCIPLE 1
KNOW YOUR AUDIENCE

Over the past few decades advertisers have become increasingly bold in the way they communicate with their audiences. Opposite page: Smint, 2000s. Previous spread: Häagen-Dazs, 1990s (detail)

Advertising is as simple as ABC – or perhaps it would be more pertinent to say ABC1 (the highest-spending socioeconomic group). Which is not to suggest, of course, that all ads are aimed principally at wealthy professionals, but rather that all successful ads are aimed at *someone in particular* – that is, a carefully defined group of one sort or another. Properly targeted ads will, both visually and verbally, speak the language of this group.

Well-researched ads speak the language of their target audience. This page: Tango, 2009. Opposite: Pepsi, 1970s

Getting customers to tell you about themselves

Market research is a complicated business which has undergone significant methodological evolution since its emergence as a stand-alone discipline in the US at the beginning of the last century. Within an advertising agency, account planners are tasked with carrying out this research. Using a variety of techniques – primary and secondary, qualitative and quantitative – they seek to enter the mind-set of particular groups of consumers, trying to discover what they think and care about, how they communicate with one another and what sort of emotional cues they are most likely to respond to. Account planners analyse data about consumers' attitudes to the client and its competitors as well as more general trends in the marketplace. The information they glean from all this will then mould every aspect of the advertising campaign, from the imagery and language it uses to the specific locations where it will appear.

Different attributes of the target audience need to be considered: for example, age, sex, education, cultural background, income. Qualitative research aims to tap into how consumers think or feel and often takes the form of focus groups, whereas quantitative research is carried out via such methods as questionnaires and is concerned with answering more fact-based questions (what, when, where, how often?). The point of all this is that, since advertising is always aimed at a particular group of people, it is much easier to create a campaign that effectively taps into those people's hopes and dreams if you know everything you can about them before the avowedly 'creative' work begins. For instance, ads aimed at the youth – or middle-youth – market will inevitably try to infiltrate

Lipsmackinthirst
quenchinacetast
inmotivatingood
buzzincooltalkin
highwalkinfastliv
inevergivin
coolfizzin PEPSI

the adolescent mind-set to help the campaign achieve a degree of playground 'cool' – always a slippery category. Pepsi's famous 'Lipsmackinthirstquenchin' slogans, one of the longest ever used in an advertising campaign, was created in the early 1970s to strike a chord with youth audiences. Tapping into the anarchic wit of teenagers, the 1990s Tango 'Orange Man' ads helped turn a previously unfashionable drink into a cult brand, a strategy that has been successfully sustained. In trying to connect with different target groups of consumers, the language employed in ads has become noticeably more diverse and segmented over the past decades – the words employed will be as off-putting to some as they are attractive to others.

Getting customers to tell you about the product

The research stage also offers an opportunity to find out how consumers actually view a particular product – rather than how the manufacturer might fondly like to think they view it. Is it seen as a functional necessity or as a luxury? As a high-quality or an economy offering? It's important to investigate such perceptions carefully, as again the findings will feed into the creative concept (see Principle 2), especially if the goal of a campaign is to change such attitudes to a given product, as was the case with the celebrated 1990s Häagen-Dazs campaign which set out to recast a traditional children's or family treat – ice cream – as an altogether more grown-up pleasure.

Nor does consumer research end when the initial findings are delivered and the creatives become involved. Although the success of a campaign may be demonstrated in the most direct terms – commercial returns – it's still essential to evaluate the effectiveness of a campaign in other respects so that the information can be used in future advertising. Focus groups and other kinds of market research are as vital at the end of an advertising campaign (in the form of post-testing) as they are at the beginning.

Ice cream has been sold in different ways to different target groups. The rarely alluded-to erotic possibilities of ice cream were placed centre stage in the Häagen-Dazs campaign, which targeted a new audience. Clockwise from top left: Häagen-Dazs, 1990s. Ben & Jerry's, 2010 and 2006. Howard Johnson's, 1951

Market research is crucial in shaping advertising campaigns as well as in developing new products or making them more responsive to consumers' needs and desires. Dulux, 1990s

Forecasting the future

Knowledge of the target audience feeds not only into the advertising campaign but also on occasion into product development. Jan Pester, former Planning Director at FCB who now runs her own marketing and research consultancy, explains: 'At the end of the 1960s two different people – Stephen King at J. Walter Thompson and Stanley Pollitt at BMP – came up with the idea of planning, which is basically about putting the consumer at the heart of the message. There are two distinct sorts of planner: those who spend most of their time sitting and working with the creatives, and those who do a bit of that but who also think about the long term and how the market might develop and what consumers might want in the future.' Pester was instrumental in one particularly successful example of the latter kind of 'future forecasting' or trend analysis: 'Some years ago I was working for Dulux, and their margins were being squeezed by own-brand competitors because it was difficult to show what was different about Dulux's white paint. So we talked to consumers and looked at different markets in different countries. And as a result of that we identified a gap in the market, which was "Not Quite White" – white with a hint of cream or pink, etc. It started something new and developed in a few years to account for 15 per cent of the paint market. Planning is about that too.'

Creamy Dulux Gloss.
For Silthane toughness and a depth of
beauty no non-drip could ever achieve.

A finish that's richer, deeper, more perfect than any non-drip gloss can give you.

A tough Silthane finish—ICI Silthane is harder-wearing than polyurethane or vinyl.

Come on. Discover the rewards of creamy, manageable Dulux Gloss Finish. To make your home feel new again.

Dulux Gloss Finish 'Trafalgar'

PRINCIPLE 2
BEHIND EVERY GREAT ADVERTISING CAMPAIGN IS A GREAT CREATIVE CONCEPT

PRINCIPLE 2:
BEHIND EVERY GREAT ADVERTISING CAMPAIGN IS A GREAT CREATIVE CONCEPT

The heart of any advertising campaign is the creative concept – the 'big idea' – which is generated from a mixture of the research into the target audience outlined in Principle 1 and a knowledge of the product or service that is being advertised. Since people generally buy something when they believe that it will benefit them in some way, it's important to make a list of the product's benefits to the consumer. The creative team – usually an art director and copywriter, following the model developed by Doyle Dane Bernbach in the 1960s – are responsible for coming up with this concept. Although in theory the art director concerns him/herself with the visual side of things while the copywriter takes care of the verbal element, such a strict division of labour doesn't always operate in practice, and particularly not in the initial stages of work.

This visually dashing series of ads from 2007 aimed to give the *Financial Times* – a specialist financial paper – a bold new profile

We live in
FINANCIAL TIMES

Mergers and Acquisitions.
In-depth coverage.

We live in **FINANCIAL TIMES**

The Rolls-Royce Silver Cloud—$13,995

"At 60 miles an hour the loudest noise in this new Rolls-Royce comes from the electric clock"

*What __makes__ Rolls-Royce the best car in the world? "There is really no magic about it—
it is merely patient attention to detail," says an eminent Rolls-Royce engineer.*

1. "At 60 miles an hour the loudest noise comes from the electric clock," reports the Technical Editor of THE MOTOR. Three mufflers tune out sound frequencies—acoustically.

2. Every Rolls-Royce engine is run for seven hours at full throttle before installation, and each car is test-driven for hundreds of miles over varying road surfaces.

3. The Rolls-Royce is designed as an *owner-driven* car. It is eighteen inches shorter than the largest domestic cars.

4. The car has power steering, power brakes and automatic gear-shift. It is very easy to drive and to park. No chauffeur required.

5. The finished car spends a week in the final test-shop, being fine-tuned. Here it is subjected to 98 separate ordeals. For example, the engineers use a *stethoscope* to listen for axle-whine.

6. The Rolls-Royce is guaranteed for *three years*. With a new network of dealers and parts-depots from Coast to Coast, service is no problem.

7. The Rolls-Royce radiator has never changed, except that when Sir Henry Royce died in 1933 the monogram RR was changed from red to black.

8. The coachwork is given five coats of primer paint, and hand rubbed between each coat, before *nine* coats of finishing paint go on.

9. By moving a switch on the steering column, you can adjust the shock-absorbers to suit road conditions.

10. A picnic table, veneered in French walnut, slides out from under the dash. Two more swing out behind the front seats.

11. You can get such optional extras as an Espresso coffee-making machine, a dictating machine, a bed, hot and cold water for washing, an electric razor or a telephone.

12. There are three separate systems of power brakes, two hydraulic and one mechanical. Damage to one system will not affect the others. The Rolls-Royce is a very *safe* car—and also a very *lively* car. It cruises serenely at eighty-five. Top speed is in excess of 100 m.p.h.

13. The Bentley is made by Rolls-Royce. Except for the radiators, they are identical motor cars, manufactured by the same engineers in the same works. People who feel diffident about driving a Rolls-Royce can buy a Bentley.

PRICE. The Rolls-Royce illustrated in this advertisement—f.o.b. principal ports of entry—costs **$13,995.**

If you would like the rewarding experience of driving a Rolls-Royce or Bentley, write or telephone to one of the dealers listed on the opposite page.

Rolls-Royce Inc., 10 Rockefeller Plaza, New York 20, N. Y., CIrcle 5-1144.

Mixing logic and magic

How the concept is plucked from this stew of information about audience and benefits is ultimately mysterious and equates to inspiration – advertising, creatives will tell you, is always a mixture of logic and magic. David Ogilvy, who started out selling stoves door-to-door in Scotland before eventually going on to oversee a worldwide network of agencies, explained his working method as follows: 'Before I sit down to do an advertising campaign I spend an awful lot of time studying the product and getting to know a lot about it. I do a lot of research. I stuff my conscious mind with information, then unhook my rational thought process and put it out of my mind. You can help this process by taking a hot bath, or a long walk, or by having dinner and drinking half a bottle of claret. I've always found that very helpful. Suddenly I get a telegram from my unconscious that says "Got an idea for you... how about this?" It has to be a relevant idea, so my unconscious has to be well-informed.'

Making it memorable – *and* relevant

Relevance is crucial, of course. Advertising costs a lot of money, so it's hardly surprising that a great deal of time and effort has also gone into devising ways to assess its effectiveness in influencing consumer behaviour as precisely as possible. For advertisers, RoI (Return on Investment) is king, and a variety of more or less scientific methods have been developed to evaluate how any given advertising campaign has achieved its goal. In the 1950s, a method known as Day-After-Recall (DAR) began to be widely used to test the memorability of TV ads by measuring the percentage of viewers who could recall having seen them 24 hours after they had been screened. However, evidence gathered subsequently suggested a poor correlation between DAR and the bottom line: that is, the fact that an ad is memorable doesn't mean that it will generate sales on behalf of the advertiser. A distinction thus came to be drawn between what

Emphasising what makes a product unique and different from its competitors is at the heart of good advertising. To do this, creatives need to know their products inside out, as David Ogilvy famously did in creating this advertising classic for Rolls-Royce, 1958 (opposite) and in this 1960s poster promoting tourism in France

WRITE THE FUTURE

nikefootball.com

might be called the attention-getting power of a particular piece of work and its 'brand linkage' – that is, how relevant the idea is to the product being advertised. Being 'creative' is not enough. 'Advertising is about communicating effectively to the consumer what your point of difference is, and why it matters,' says Jan Pester. 'It's making your point of difference relevant and motivating to the consumer.' Digital technology and the new twenty-first-century model for brand-consumer relations have made it possible to measure the effectiveness of campaigns much more precisely (see Principle 6).

ESP and the brand

It was Rosser Reeves of the Ted Bates agency who developed the idea of the USP, or 'unique selling proposition', in the 1950s. USP theory assumes that an ad should communicate a message based on the principal quality that differentiates a product from its rivals in the marketplace. The difficulty with this, however, is that products are rarely unique in terms of quality or performance – or if they are at first, thanks to a phenomenon known as 'market convergence', whereby competing products are quickly adapted to match any innovations, they rarely remain so for long. In some degree, then, the USP has come to be replaced by what has been termed the ESP, or 'emotional selling proposition', which focuses on giving the product a unique 'personality'. This will usually be based on a 'brand truth'. 'Brand', of course, is a key term in marketing speak. The American Marketing Association defines it as meaning a 'name, term, design, symbol, or any

Does exactly what it says on the tin.

other feature that identifies one seller's good or service as distinct from those of other sellers' – it's what sets a particular producer or supplier apart from its rivals, the quality that gives it a unique identity in the marketplace. The brand is therefore the basis of the ESP.

Experienced creatives will tell you that the best way to get a feel for the product is to do some serious homework: read all the technical brochures and go to the factory where it's made and talk to the people who actually make it. It's also important to look at the advertising generated by competing brands. Why do they think consumers want to buy their product? Is there a reason – a potential USP/ESP – why those same consumers might or ought to choose yours instead? David Ogilvy again: 'The more you know about it, the more likely you are to come up with a big idea for selling it. When I got the Rolls-Royce account, I spent three weeks reading about the car and came across a statement that "at sixty miles an hour, the loudest noise comes from the electric clock." This became the headline, and it was followed by 607 words of factual copy.' And so, from three weeks of intensive research and a single stroke of inspiration, was born one of the most admired and iconic ads of the twentieth century.

Few brands are more famous than Nike, and few logos are as instantly recognisable as Nike's 'swoosh'. Hardly less successful in communicating the company's USP is Ronseal's famous 'Does what it says on the tin' slogan

The morning after test

Having come up with a concept that they like, the art director and copywriter might employ one of a range of devices or rules-of-thumb commonly used to assess its suitability. The first of these is the 'overnight test' – what may look wonderful in the heat of the moment, or at the end of a gruelling day of brainstorming, may not seem quite so smart the following morning. If the idea still sparkles in the cold light of day, however, it has just jumped an important first hurdle. Some creatives also use the objectivity test contained in the acronym 'SIMPLES', which asks whether the idea has the following qualities: is it S = sympathetic; I = individual; M = memorable; P = pertinent to the product; L = light/fresh in tone; E = economical in its use of production techniques; and, finally and crucially, S = surprising? If an idea can *objectively* – and that's the hard part – be said to fulfil all these criteria, it's probably worth pursuing further.

Despite all of these internal checks and assessments, there's sometimes a suspicion that adverts – certain kinds of adverts at any rate – have been conceived to draw the approbation of the ad maker's peers rather than to capture the attention of the target consumer group. They're self-advertisingly clever, perhaps quirky – but it's not always clear what they're supposed to be about, apart from themselves. Speak to an account manager – the person usually responsible for selling the creative team's idea to the client – and you'll quickly become aware of the potential for internal agency disharmony over such matters. Clients – the people who actually pay for the work, after all – are ultimately concerned with the commercial benefits generated by campaigns, but account managers may sometimes come to feel that their creatives are less focused on this fact than on capturing one of the numerous prestigious awards that are doled out annually by professional advertising bodies such as the New York Art Directors Club in the US and the Designers and Art Directors Association (D&AD) in Britain, or at the influential Cannes Lions Festival.

Few TV spots have proved as
memorable as the much-parodied
series featuring businessman
Victor Kiam advertising the shaving
products of his own company
Remington and launching 'I liked
it so much, I bought the company'
as one of the all-time-great
commercial slogans

An eye on the prize?

D&AD held its first awards ceremony in 1962, at a time when advertising was growing in importance and influence, and being in receipt of one of D&AD's famous Yellow Pencils or being included in its Annual soon became a crucial mark of peer respect for creatives. The impact was decisive, though not always beneficial. As the British advertising industry commentator Jeremy Bullmore has put it: 'D&AD probably did more good than harm but it certainly did a great deal of harm. It instilled a false sense of value in a particular kind of creative work that wasn't necessarily the best type of work commercially. It allowed many advertising people to convince themselves that they were fine artists as opposed to people working in a commercial business.' And, as said above, advertising should always be about the client's bottom line.

Originality, of course, is rightly a prized quality in advertising, as it is in most creative industries, but it's dangerous when that originality becomes self-serving, or when it fails to underscore the particular qualities of the product it is trying to promote. A good example is the moody postwar 'You're Never Alone with a Strand' cigarette ad,

which was regarded as avant-garde for the way it favoured existential atmospherics over message. Its impact on the smokers' market wasn't favourable, however, in part because its message appeared to be, on the contrary, 'You're *always* alone with a Strand'.

There's a whole category of ads sometimes known as 'naff classics' that would never earn their makers a D&AD Yellow Pencil but that have proved remarkably successful in selling the product in question: the 1979 Victor Kiam Remington ad, which turned 'I liked it so much I bought the company' into a national catchphrase, for instance, or the surreally kitsch Ferrero Rocher 'Ambassador's Parties' campaign. Both nonetheless acquired that ineffable quality of 'fame' for their products.

On the other hand, an ad agency that concentrates only on hardline 'retail' work – producing none-too-glamorous ads that usually pay most of the bills – and finds no time to create work that promotes its more floridly creative capacities probably won't survive for very long. Industry prestige is vital, even if the work that garners it isn't always the most successful in purely commercial terms.

Sometimes so-called 'naff classics' have succeeded where cooler, more voguish bits of advertising have failed. This page: Ferrero Rocher, 1993. Opposite: Strand, 1959

PRINCIPLE 3
LESS IS MORE

PRINCIPLE 3:
LESS IS MORE

Bold, surreal juxtapositions – a baby holding a razor blade, for instance – deliver strong, consciousness-altering messages. Gillette, 1905

The more information you put into an ad, the less people are likely to take away from it. As Frank Lowe, one-time head of pioneering UK agency Collett Dickenson Pearce, put it: 'Bad advertising tends to be complex advertising. Make it clean and simple. It's the old analogy that if you throw five tennis balls at somebody, they can't catch any of them. But if you throw only one, they can.' A particular product or service may be better than its rivals in a hundred ways, but the ad that best conveys that superiority is likely to home in on just one of those qualities – its USP or ESP if you like – and to express it as simply and memorably as possible, as in this surprising and magnificently to-the-point advert for Gillette (shown opposite), which was conceived to introduce the new concept of safety razorblades to a still-sceptical market.

Think small.

Think small, think differently: advertising often aims to change the way consumers think about a particular product by making unexpected (and perhaps even seemingly anti-commercial) statement or offering striking visual analogies. This page: Volkswagen Beetle, 1961. Opposite: Boddingtons, 1990s

Positioning your product

Positioning is key. Ted Morgan defines it as follows: 'Essentially, it's like finding a seat on a crowded bus. You look at the market place. You see what vacancy there is. You build your campaign to position your product in that vacancy. If you do it right, the straphangers won't be able to grab your seat.' Doyle Dane Bernbach's groundbreaking Volkswagen ads from the early 1960s involved a masterful piece of positioning, avoiding the hype and hyperbole usually associated with car advertising to address the viewer with self-deprecating humour. 'To advertise a car that looked like an orthopedic boot would have defeated me,' David Ogilvy commented. 'But Bill Bernbach and his merry men positioned Volkswagen as a protest against the vulgarity of Detroit cars in those days, thereby making the Beetle a cult among those Americans who eschew conspicuous consumption.'

Homing in effectively on the point of difference that really makes the product stand out from its competitors is often best achieved by means of a little lateral thinking. For instance, when London agency Bartle Bogle Hegarty was called in to help relaunch Boddingtons, a brand of bitter originally brewed in Manchester, it applied a bit of transformatory creative logic to the idea of the beer's creaminess. As the managing director of Boddingtons' parent group explained: 'We were thinking how to turn a second-rate north-west brand into something more stylish, to make it more appealing again. BBH thought of focusing on the creamy aspect, of selling a beer like a face cream.' And so it was that a series of award-winning ads were born that drew an analogy between beer and face cream, ice cream, sun cream and whipped cream. The sense of local identity was retained both in the tagline 'The Cream of Manchester' and, in the television campaign, in the use of a series of attractive women with distinctive Northern accents. Giving a simple, relevant idea – Bovril gives you energy, tomato ketchup is made from actual tomatoes, Ribena is an essentially natural product, drinking a particular brand of spring water makes you feel vital and young, you are what you eat – a clear, visually inventive treatment is the key to a great deal of effective, memorable advertising.

No one grows Ketchup like Heinz.

evian.
Live young

Maria Sharapova
Wimbledon Champion

Official bottled water of Wimbledon

THE CHAMPIONSHIPS
WIMBLEDON

Previous spread: Clear messages
given simple but striking visual
treatments make for memorable
advertising. Bovril, 1930s;
Heinz, 2007. This page: Ajinomoto,
2006; Evian, 2011; Ribena, 2010

Opposite page: When it comes
to writing great catchphrases,
simplicity is a virtue. Top: Heinz,
1970s. Bottom: Smash, 1974

Some catchphrases manage to make seemingly inimitable use of the most common items of vocabulary; others play fast and loose with 'proper' grammar. Top: Mars, 2009. Bottom: Milk, 1958

The right catchphrase

Gray Jolliffe, the copywriter at the London agency Boase Massimi Pollitt who came up with the classic 'For Mash Get Smash' tagline, which – along with some splendidly tinpot Martians – helped to turn a brand of instant mashed potato into a bestseller and turned Jolliffe himself into something of an icon of his trade, later said of his most famous piece of work: 'I'm not proud of it. I'm just embarrassed by anyone thinking that it's important.' It's true that, as a phrase, it lacks many traditional literary qualities, but like all the best advertising slogans it has an irresistible simplicity and catchiness – and simplicity and catchiness are two of the most important qualities in advertising. The slogan 'Beanz Meanz Heinz' drew complaints from schoolteachers when it was first deployed in the 1960s on account of its creative misspelling, just as 'Drinka Pinta Milka Day' had done the previous decade, but proved memorable enough to be voted the most popular advertising slogan ever in 1999. As one commentator has noted, it had the immediacy of graffiti and 'just enough grammatical anarchy to earn a place in the popular idiom'. Like 'For Mash Get Smash' after it, it also made a whole category of food synonymous with a single brand.

The best catchphrases and slogans have often taken on a life of their own beyond the campaigns that first launched them into the public consciousness. The 1984 'Where's the beef?' ads created for the Wendy's fast-food chain turned Clara Peller into a national icon at the age of 81 as well as giving Walter Mondale a memorable putdown to aim at his presidential rival, Senator Gary Hart, in a live television debate the same year. 'When I hear your new ideas, I'm reminded of that ad, "Where's the beef?"' the former Democratic vice-president spat at Hart. The Wendy's advertising campaign was revived in 2011, while the phrase has become a staple of political debate.

Though simple in appearance, successful slogans are often surprisingly bold. Launching a catchphrase is mined with risks. What if no one gets it? What if people just think it silly? The German phrase 'Vorsprung durch Technik' has entered the English language since it was first used in an Audi ad in 1984. Discovered on a sign hanging in an Audi

factory in Germany, the words were seized on as a suitable slogan despite the fact that most Britons have a very limited understanding of German and, certainly in the early 1980s, perhaps (given how many would have personally experienced the deprivations and worse of World War II) a degree of anti-German prejudice. Emphasising the product's origins thus took a certain amount of courage. There was a danger that 'Vorsprung Durch Technik' might have been met with blank incomprehension or worse by the English-speaking public, just as 'Beanz Meanz Heinz' might have been dismissed as mere nursery-rhyme inanity instead of becoming indelibly imprinted on the consciousness of more or less every UK resident across almost half a century. Successful advertising often demands the bravery to take a chance and risk failure. It follows, then, that the boldness necessary to create genuinely memorable ads depends in large part on a strong bond of trust between agency and client.

A little jingle

The jingle (often little more than a slogan set to music) is one of the most powerful tricks of the TV ad maker's trade. The best have proved surprisingly enduring. Cliff Adams's 'Murraymints – the too-good-to-hurry mints' was actually one

Occasionally slogans go on to have a life beyond the advertising campaign that brought them into being. 'Where's the beef?' quickly entered the language of national politics in the US. Wendy's, 1984

Even spectacular ads that look as
though they were costly or physically
challenging to make usually have a
simple message at their core. This
page: Maxell, 1980s. Opposite, top:
Sony, 1995; bottom: Sony Bravia, 2005

of the very first jingles to feature in an ad in the UK; over
50 years later, it is still instantly recognisable. 'A Mars a day
helps you work, rest and play' (debuted in 1959) remains
equally fresh; it's so familiar it doesn't even have to be used
in full any more. Simplicity and directness of expression
are great virtues in jingle writing. There's a story about how
Johnny Johnston, aka the 'King of the Jingles', came up with
his jingle for Rael Brook Toplin shirts. 'What's so special
about your shirts?' Johnston quizzed manufacturer Harry
Rael Brook directly. 'You don't need to iron them,' came the
response, whereupon Johnston sat down at his piano and sang
the words 'Rael Brook Toplin, the shirts you don't iron!' three
times, before moving into a different key and singing them
again. 'That's what I want! Don't change anything!' Rael Brook
is reported to have cried out at once, delighted. Job done.
Advertising can be a delightfully simple business – sometimes.

Spectacular can still be simple

Even the most elaborate or breathtakingly spectacular ads
usually have a very simple message at their core. For instance,
the 1995 'Armchair' campaign for Sony's surround-sound TV,
conceived by British ad agency Boase Massimi Pollitt, set new
standards for the daring of its execution. It involved a besuited
man jumping from a helicopter at 12,000 feet and hurtling
towards the Earth – somewhat surreally – in an armchair. It
was both difficult and expensive to make, but it delivered a
crystal-clear message – that surround-sound TV makes the
viewer experience the world with greater immediacy – with
imaginative flair and maximum visceral impact. A well-known
long-running campaign for Maxell had used a similar idea.
To underline the colour quality of its Bravia high-definition
televisions and associated products, Sony commissioned an
advert involving thousands of coloured balls swarming along a
San Francisco street. The balls featured were real, rather than
computer-generated, so the execution was elaborate, but the
message was simplicity itself – 'Colour like no other,' as the
tagline had it.

PRINCIPLE 4
A PICTURE IS WORTH A THOUSAND WORDS – BUT NEVER UNDERESTIMATE THE POWER OF A GREAT HEADLINE

Take a minute to refresh

Coca-Cola has the charm of purity. It is prepared with the finished art that comes from a lifetime of practice. Its delicious taste never loses the freshness of appeal that first delighted you...always bringing you a cool, clean sense of complete refreshment. Thirst asks nothing more.

When you're so busy you're ready to drop...drop into an easy chair and enjoy *the pause that refreshes* with a frosty bottle of Coca-Cola from your own refrigerator. It's a refreshing little minute that's long enough for a big rest.

Drink
Coca-Cola
Delicious and Refreshing
5¢

THE PAUSE THAT REFRESHES

Campaigns increasingly aim to cross linguistic borders without the need for regional variations of the kind seen in these adverts. Top: Coca-Cola, Italy, 1930s. Bottom: Coca-Cola, US, 1942

"Rinfresco!"

Coca-Cola

PRINCIPLE 4
A PICTURE IS WORTH A THOUSAND WORDS – BUT NEVER UNDERESTIMATE THE POWER OF A GREAT HEADLINE

Most adverts contain both words and pictures. But the relationship between these core elements has changed radically over the past century. As manufacturers moved away from the idea that the best way of persuading people to buy their product was to make a super-rational appeal to them by listing *all of* that product's virtues, so text began to give place to evocative imagery designed to persuade viewers at a more subliminal level. Dreamy, soft-focus photography thus came to be adopted to suggest the sensuous pleasures of a wide range of products, from bath towels to alcoholic beverages. The shift away from words has been further accelerated by twenty-first-century economic globalisation. With manufacturers and corporations keen to create one-size-fits-all campaigns that can be deployed worldwide, adverts are increasingly becoming image-led in an attempt to transcend language barriers and do away with regional or national variations.

Some ads really don't need words
– beyond the company name and
contact details – to convey their
message. FedEx, 2010. Opposite
clockwise: BMW,1990s;
LILA, 2000s; Lego Toys,1970s

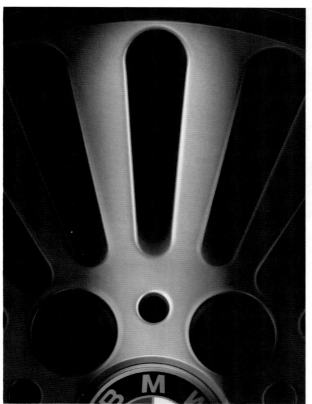

You can't always spot a hazard but a BMW wheel can. Black ice, wet leaves, loose stones. What your eyesight can easily miss hasn't escaped the foresight of our engineers at BMW. The result is the concept of intelligent wheels. For us, roadholding is nothing short of an obsession. Equally important is our belief that the most important component of any car is the driver. Since the wheels are the car and driver's sole contact with the road, we design them to provide both with the most accurate feedback. How? By a combination of stability and traction control systems linked to the car's engine management system. The wheels can identify potential hazards and, in just 17 milliseconds, activate the appropriate response. A reaction time 40 times faster than most drivers. So not only do the wheels spend more time in touch with the road, you do too. Intelligent wheels from BMW. Arguably one of the greatest inventions since, well, the wheel.

BMW Information, P.O. BOX 161, Croydon, Surrey CR9 1QB. 0800 325600. http://www.bmw.co.uk

The Ultimate Driving Machine

Keep on feeding their imagination.

Few toys feed a child's imagination more than LEGO bricks.

It develops their co-ordination, dexterity, creativity and sense of design – giving them a chance to work alone or express themselves and their experiences with other children, and you.

To make it easier for you to hand out a suitable mix of bricks, we've sorted LEGO out into three boxes – each box designed for a different age group.

Box 1040 for Nursery and Playgroups. Box 1045 for children up to six. Box 1050 for six year olds and over. Each of these boxes contains enough bricks for six children to play with.

We've also designed a range of seven supplementary sets which can be added to these boxes.

Go on, give them second helpings. Order more LEGO.

LEGO

LEGO IS A NEW TOY EVERY DAY.

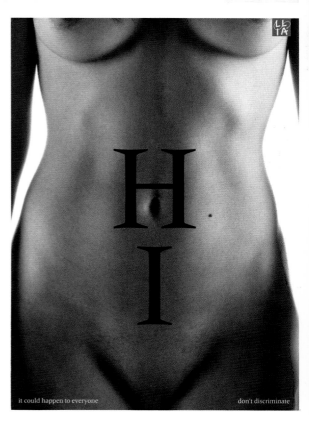

it could happen to everyone   don't discriminate

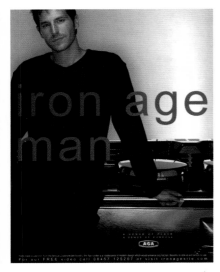

The best advertising is a perfect blend of verbal and visual elements. Economy of means should always be the watchword. This page: Aga, 2000s; Sunday Times, 2011. Opposite from top: Virgin Atlantic, 2000s; Heineken, 1990s; Apple MacBook, 2008

Nonetheless, the dialogue between word and image remains at the heart of great advertising. Ideally, verbal and visual elements should complement, rather than repeat, one another. A headline that completes the thought begun in the picture, or vice versa, is always more satisfying than an ad where the whole message is contained in just one element, with the second element reduced to a mere supporting role.

Setting a puzzle

How obvious should a campaign be? Therein lies one of the great arts of advertising. Obviously adverts that are so obscure as to be incomprehensible will fail in their mission, but a little mystery can be very useful indeed, and the space between headline and image is ideally suited to creating a small enigma. The image may confound the expectations set up in the headline text, or the latter might suggest a twist on the image. The most successful ads often demand a little work on the part of their audience. As Frank Lowe put it: 'Ads should meet the consumer at a point halfway between the printed page or TV screen and the consumer's brain. The consumer knows you're playing a game and he can bring a lot to your ad. Having done a bit of work on it – like everything else in life – the pleasure of understanding the ad is all the greater.' Forcing the viewer to complete the idea – a bit like solving a crossword puzzle clue, or guessing the punchline to a joke – creates complicity between advertiser and audience. Making sure that the puzzle is neither too easy nor too difficult is the hard part. Together headline and picture should form an intriguing but ultimately clear whole.

Sit, shower, shave.

upper class *New Revivals Lounge.*

virgin atlantic

This poster needs refreshment. All those in favour say "i."

Thinnovation.

The world's thinnest notebook. 13.3" widescreen display. Full-sized keyboard. **MacBook** Air

DUBONNET

DUBONNET

DUBONNET
VIN TONIQUE
AU QUINQUINA

Be careful
what you say
+ where you
say it!

CARELESS TALK
COSTS LIVES

Miss Dior

Definitely, very Dior

Miss Dior by the world famous house of Christian Dior.
Perfume. Eau de Toilette. Cologne. From 6.00 to 42.00.

Dior

A great illustrator can immediately
give a campaign a distinctive look.
Clockwise from top: A.M. Cassandre,
Dubonnet, 1930s. René Gruau,
Christian Dior, 1970; Fougasse
(Cyril Kenneth Bird), Ministry of
Information, 1940s

More classic illustrators. Clockwise from top left: Jules Chéret, Paris Courses, 1900s; Saul Bass, Anatomy of a Murder, 1959; Abram Games, Grow Your Own Food, 1940s

THE LONGER YOU LIVE ON THE STREET
THE HARDER IT IS TO GET OFF IT | **samusocial**

SUPPORT US AT WWW.SAMUSOCIAL

You'll never be surprised on road again.
The Electronic brake assist system of CC.

Das Auto.

Drawing the eye

And then, of course, what sort of picture? As the twentieth century progressed, photography increasingly displaced hand-drawn imagery in print advertising, but a talented illustrator has always been able to bring a distinctive visual feel – and perhaps a kind of fantasy difficult to achieve thanks to the inherent realism of photography as a medium – to a campaign. Such uniqueness is invaluable in advertising, where the goal is always to be able to draw the eye – elegantly perhaps, but unerringly – to one's own message amidst the surrounding visual clutter. Illustrators such as A.M. Cassandre, René Gruau, Fougasse (Cyril Kenneth Bird), especially in his work for the Ministry of Information during World War II, Jules Chéret, Saul Bass and Abram Games created some of the most memorable and effective advertising material ever produced. In the wake of the advent of digital imaging and computer manipulation, the division between photography and illustration has become increasingly blurred.

Thanks to computers and increasingly sophisticated image-manipulation techniques, visual ideas that would once have required the skills of an illustrator can increasingly be given photorealistic treatments. Left: Samusocial, 2010. Above: Volkswagen, 2011

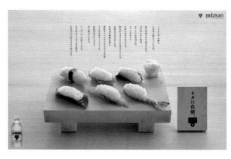

This is the woman. She is knowing we are looking.

FRENCH CONNECTION **FOR WOMAN**

There are always new and unusual ways to express ideas. Surprise – whether visual or visual – is one of the grails of advertisers. This page, clockwise from top right: Selfridges, 2009; Mizkan; French Connection, 2010. Opposite: World Wildlife Fund, 2008

NO MORE FISH IN THE SEA?

PROJECT OCEAN.

Help us to protect our oceans and change the way we eat.
Find out more and join the campaign at **selfridges.com/projectocean**

ZSL
LIVING CONSERVATION

SELFRIDGES&C⁹

Try to surprise

No one wants to produce visual muzak. Surprise is one of the most important effects an advert can achieve – something the climate change poster here certainly manages. Visually this can be accomplished by showing an object or scene from an unusual angle, or using an unwonted crop or layout, as with this dynamic Selfridges poster, to make the familiar seem unfamiliar or showing it in an unfamiliar way. The reversal of visual expectations in the food ad on page 69 makes its point powerfully – great sushi is in large part dependent on how you prepare the rice, the part of the dish that's usually half-concealed in shots of this kind. As mentioned above, forcing viewers to work the message out for themselves is a good way to capture their attention, as in the ad for extra-large condoms shown above. Adverts that make their audience feel pleased with themselves – because they've solved the puzzle or understood the joke – can help to build the bond between brand and consumer: the French Connection ad on the previous spread is particularly daring in this regard. Brand loyalty is based on this kind of complicity.

This page: Humour and allowing audiences to work visual puzzles out for themselves are both classic advertising strategies. Durex

Opposite: Hackneyed language is generally to be avoided, but clichés can be given fresh life in certain contexts. Project Ocean, 2011

Step into middle England's best loved department store, stroll through haberdashery to the audio visual department where an awfully well brought up young man will bend over backwards to find the right TV for you then go to dixons.co.uk and buy it.

Dixons.co.uk
The last place you want to go

This page: Nowadays, with so much shopping activity having gone online, the website address is sometimes the most important part of an ad. Dixons, 2009

Opposite: Reticence is out of fashion in contemporary campaigns, in contrast to the understatement of the Modess sanitary towel ad. Clockwise from top left: Harvey Nichols, 2000s; Modess, 1952; Diesel, 2010

"OH SHIT"

Hibby wears Perfectly Pink Trish McEvoy lipstick, psychedelic hot pants and halterneck top.

The life of HARVEY NICHOLS

Modess .... because

GOODBYE INHIBITIONS.

BE STUPID DIESEL

Typography can enhance the message contained in the words themselves. These ads all convey an exuberance appropriate to the products they are promoting. This page, clockwise from top: National Lottery, 2010; Kirin Beer, 1990s; Master Foods, 2000s. Opposite: Trojan, 2008

Bonding through humour

It's important to avoid clichés verbally as well as visually – although, as David Ogilvy said, 'The two most powerful words you can use in a headline are FREE and NEW.' Adverts rarely contain many words, so it's important to avoid repeating what's already been said in the headline in the body copy (the text below the headline, which usually appears in a smaller font size) – every word counts. Tone and the precise words employed will depend on the target audience – the ad should 'speak their language' – and there's probably still some truth in what Lord Peter Wimsey observed in 1933 in *Murder Must Advertise*: 'the most convincing copy [is] always written with the tongue in the cheek, a genuine conviction of the commodity's worth producing – for some reason – poverty and flatness of style.' Copy must be persuasive, but that can often be achieved more effectively through humour than by adopting a tone of plain sincerity. Though clichés are to be avoided, pertinent twists on well-known sayings or phrases can be provocative, as with 'No more fish in the sea?' (page 70).

The body copy usually contains further information about the product as well as a 'call to action', which tells the viewer what to do next – increasingly, log on to a particular website. A lot of ads end with a strapline or slogan, a short phrase that captures everything you want to convey about the brand. In terms of tone, irreverence isn't just reserved for the youth market – it can also be a high-end strategy. Whereas, in the 1950s, an ad for sanitary towels might be too polite actually to say directly what it was for, reticence is rarely practised now. For Wimsey one important lesson was: 'if, by the most far-fetched stretch of ingenuity, an indecent meaning could be read into a headline, that was the meaning that the great British Public would infallibly read into it.' In that respect, advertising has changed a great deal: people don't have to imagine indecency or profanity any more.

Finding the right font

And, of course, it's not just a question of the words themselves. Typography is hardly less important in achieving a particular effect: different fonts can project a wide range of moods, from sturdily old-fashioned to breezily or modishly contemporary to exuberantly uninhibited. This ad for Kirin beer (opposite page) takes full advantage of the foreignness of its product and makes inventive visual play with Japanese calligraphy. It's important to achieve a balance between image and typography. Often one element will be bolder than the other: if the imagery 'shouts', it might be better if the setting of the text 'whispers'. Elements should never compete for attention, but should instead have an internal hierarchy that leads the viewer's eye naturally to the ad's payoff, as with this ad for T-Mobile (shown overleaf). Consistent use of typography has become part of companies' brand identities: some advertisers are instantly identifiable just by the typeface they use, even before their logo has appeared or their name has been mentioned. Thanks to its typography, the 'Office Totty' ad hardly needs to name Mars.

The best ads demand an active response. To do this, they need to make eye contact with their audience, although not necessarily quite as directly as one of the most successful (and parodied) campaigns of all time, Lord Kitchener's 'Your Country Needs You', does (shown overleaf).

Office totty

Mars®

Pleasure you can't measure

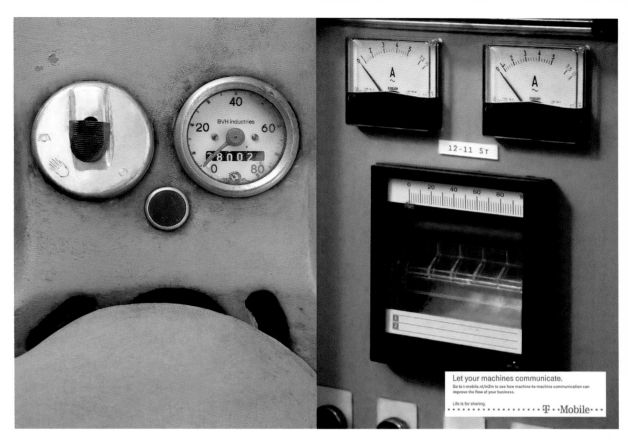

Let your machines communicate.
Go to t-mobile.nl/m2m to see how machine-to-machine communication can improve the flow of your business.

Life is for sharing.

T··Mobile··

This page: Great ads demand attention, and lead the eye unerringly through their various visual elements to the all-important payoff. T-Mobile, 2011. Lord Kitchener Recruitment Poster, 1914

Opposite: The association between Mars and a particular typographic treatment is so strong that the product hardly needs to be named

PRINCIPLE 5
ORIGINALITY IS
JUST COPYING
WITH A TWIST

PRINCIPLE 5
ORIGINALITY IS JUST COPYING WITH A TWIST

Some iconic campaigns have been endlessly copied and parodied. The famous Kitchener image shown on page 77 has been appropriated to sell mustard among many other things, while Uncle Sam has lent his finger to numerous campaigns of different political hues. Above: American Civil Liberties Union, 2007. Opposite: Colman's Mustard, 2009

'There is nothing new under the sun': this bit of wisdom is as true today as it was when the aphoristically inclined author of the biblical book of Ecclesiastes first wrote it in the third century BC. Although as an industry advertising feeds on novelty, an analysis of any campaign usually shows lines of influence from other media or even other ads. Originality, then, is often little more than a fresh twist on an old formula.

**Hamlet.
The Mild Cigar.**

The durability test

One of the most enduring formulas is the so-called 'durability test', memorably used in an innovative early series of TV ads for Timex, in which reporter John Cameron Swayze showed timepieces being subjected to extreme trials of endurance, such as a high-diver jumping into the ocean to test whether his Timex would still be working after taking the plunge. Of course, it emerged in pristine working order. 'Takes a licking and keeps on ticking' concluded the famous tagline.

Inspiration is everywhere

Legend has it that one of the greatest and longest-running TV advertising campaigns began with one of the creatives from the great Collett Dickenson Pearce agency spying a poster based on the famous 'Peanuts' comic strip from a London bus: 'Happiness is...' ran the caption. This then fed into a concept for Hamlet cigars based on the simple premise of a man getting into a tight scrape and then lighting up for consolation. 'Happiness is a cigar called Hamlet' announced a voice, to the accompaniment of Jacques Loussier's jazzed-up take on Bach's *Air on a G String*. The campaign ran in various forms from the mid-1960s to 1999, when a blanket ban on cigar advertisement finally put an end to it. The 1987 version featuring Gregor Fisher trying to cover up his bald pate as he was snapped in a photo booth was voted the best ad ever in Cannes in the mid-1990s. Inspiration is potentially to be found anywhere and everywhere. No wonder self-respecting creatives rarely venture out without a notebook.

Ideas for ads can be found anywhere, from classic tropes such as the durability test to 'Peanuts' posters. Above: Hamlet, 1987. Opposite: Timex, 1940s

Statistics and 'scientific' before-and-after shots are advertising evergreens. This page, below: Costa Coffee, 2000s. Right: Bufferin, 1950s. Opposite: Men's Dry Control Hairspray, 1971

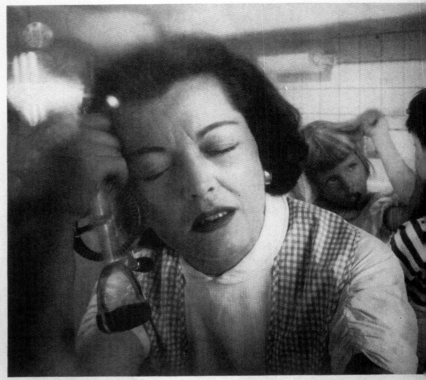

June 14, 1958

Bufferin® relieves pain twice as fast!

Di-Alminate® makes the difference

Medical science knows that a pain reliever must get into the blood stream before it can start to relieve pain.

Bufferin combines aspirin with an exclusive combination of two antacid ingredients called Di-Alminate. This speeds the pain reliever into the blood stream *twice as fast.* So . . .

Bufferin relieves pain *twice as fast.* And it won't upset your stomach as aspirin often does.

1. <u>All</u> leading pain remedies, including other compounds, rely on aspirin! But...

2. Aspirin <u>without</u> antacid is relatively slow-acting. It is acid and can irritate your stomach.

3. Only Bufferin adds to aspirin an exclusive combination of antacids called Di-Alminate. So Bufferin relieves pain <u>twice as fast</u> as aspirin—won't upset your stomach!

Won't upset your stomach as aspirin often does!

BRISTOL-MYERS' BRAND OF ALUMINUM GLYCINATE AND MAGNESIUM CARBONATE.

7 OUT OF 10 COFFEE LOVERS PREFER COSTA.

In head-to-head taste tests, 7 out of 10 coffee lovers preferred Costa cappuccino to our leading competitors.

WE MAKE IT BETTER

Pete Maravich 1967.
His hair was still wet behind the ears.

Pete Maravich 1971.
Introducing Vitalis® Dry Control.

Sure. Years ago, Pete Maravich wet his hair down with oils, grease and water. Most guys did back then.

But this is 1971. And Pete knows better. Today he likes his hair dry. No oils. No grease. No water.

So he combs his hair casual. And he knows it'll stay that way with new Vitalis Dry Control.

Dry Control is a different kind of hair groom. It's a spray that keeps your hair in place without slicking it down. It's dry. It's casual. And it's natural.

In fact, it's even more than natural. It's supernatural. Because you know it's there... but you just can't see it.

And that's what most guys want today. Unless they're still wet behind the ears.

The Supernatural.
You know it's there, you just can't see it.

Suggestive science

Advertisers love the idea of using scientific evidence to demonstrate the superiority of their product. Hard-and-fast, science-based guarantees of success can rarely be offered, although the before-and-after formula remains visually suggestive and statistics and other impressive-sounding facts and figures are regularly deployed to give a kind of scientific authority to an advertising message. One of the most iconic and instantly recognisable taglines in British advertising, Whiskas's 'Eight out of ten owners said their cats preferred it' (or 'Eight out of ten owners *who expressed a preference* said their cats preferred it', as it later became), employs a familiar formula ('8 out of 10 doctors recommend' etc) that never seems to go out of fashion – largely because it works!

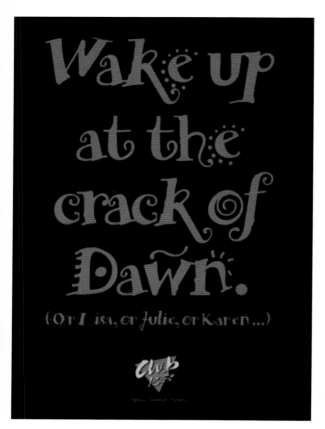

This page: Life-and-death messages can make use of humour just as successfully as other, inherently lighter enterprises. Left: Club 18-30, 1996. Right: Commonwealth Department of Community Services and Health, Aboriginal Health Workers of Australia, 1991

Opposite: Politics is rarely a laughing matter, but some commercial campaigns have made cheeky reference to politicians' foibles, while some politically engaged campaigns have employed visual wit to deliver their messages. Clockwise from top left: Stop the War Coalition, 2004; Sketchley's, 1990s; Ryanair, 2000s; Labour Party, 2005

Tap into the emotions – or feelings about class

Humour is one of advertisers' strongest suits and has been used to great effect in a variety of contexts. A knowing wink to the target audience can be very powerful, while no less explicit wit of a visual kind has been successfully deployed to deliver serious, potentially life-and-death messages. Even in a political context, especially in guerrilla campaigns, humour can be very successful. If some ads go for the funny bone, others aim for the heart. Sentimentality – often synonymous with the deployment of pets and young children – is another popular gambit. Dogs have proved particularly useful in promoting goods where a direct demonstration of the product in question using a human would be inadvisable – loo paper, for instance. Aleksandr the aristocratically styled Russian meerkat, the (CGI-generated) face of www.comparethemarket.com, has become a commercial phenomenon in his own right, even publishing a highly successful autobiography. Words with emotional connotations have a proven power in headline

MAKE TEA NOT WAR

STOP THE WAR COALITION
www.stopwar.org.uk

KARMARAMA

IF ONLY SHE HAD GONE TO SKETCHLEY...

Sketchley

We know the meaning of cleaning

WARNING
THE TORIES COULD SERIOUSLY DAMAGE YOUR ECONOMY

Labour
www.labour.org.uk

(Publicité)

RYANAIR
POUR TOUTES LES OCCASIONS

Avec Ryanair, toute ma famille peut venir assister à mon mariage

100.000 BILLETS
NE PAYEZ QUE LES TAXES ET CHARGES

VOYAGEZ EN FÉVRIER ET MARS '08   RÉSERVEZ JUSQU'A JEUDI

HÔTELS À PRIX RÉDUITS, À PARTIR DE €17 SEULEMENT SUR WWW.RYANAIRHOTELS.COM

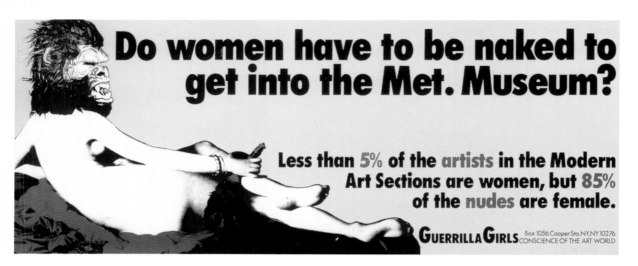

Animals are usually employed in ads for their cosy associations. The Guerrilla Girls' use of gorilla masks marks a notable exception. This page: Andrex, 2010. Opposite, top: Guerrilla Girls, 1980s. Bottom: comparethemarket.com, 2009

Class has been crucial in many advertising campaigns. Above: Bird's Eye, 1974. Opposite: After Eight, 1970s

writing. It's hardly surprising that ads should also frequently tap into social ambitions: aspirationalism would certainly appear to be behind this campaign for 'After Eights' mints (shown opposite) – are the sort of people shown in the picture really the target audience for the product? The same point could be made of the famously successful Ferrero Rocher 'Ambassador's Parties' campaign discussed earlier. Feelings about class have been profitably exploited in the opposite direction too: in what appeared a revolutionary coup at the time, Alan Parker cast children who spoke with strong regional accents for his 1970s TV ads for Bird's Eye which showed a boy and girl bonding over beef burgers (above). The manufacturer received letters of complaint about the accents but the campaign was a hit. It dared to speak the non-RP dialect of its target audience in a way that few, if any, screen ads had done before.

"As Lucinda so rightly points out, it's the only envelope that doesn't require an outrageously expensive stamp this Christmas…"

Daddy, what did YOU do in the Great War?

The promise of pleasure, or at least personal benefit, underlies most adverts, but some use threats and bribes to startling effect. Opposite, top: Heineken, 2004. Bottom: HM Revenue and Customs, 2007. This page: Recruitment poster, 1915

Threats and bribery

Though adverts usually work on the premise that their product will make your life better – aspiration is built into advertising – in some (usually non-commercial) contexts, guilt has been used to dramatic effect, such as in the 1915 army recruitment poster 'Daddy, What Did *You* Do in the Great War?'. The sands of time running out might be considered a dangerously alarming image in an advertising context, but instilling a mild sense of disquiet in viewers is probably justifiable if you want to urge them to hurry up with their tax returns. Blackmail was the apparent strategy of an irreverent and highly ironic series of TV ads for a popular brand of lager featuring an expanding cast of celebrities the public loved to hate singing off-key. 'Buy a pint of Heineken or we'll keep running this commercial,' threatened the first of four ads; the fourth maintained the 'or else' tone of menace.

Film icons from Laurel and Hardy to James Bond have inspired advertising campaigns. This page: Holsten Pils, 1983. Opposite, top: PG Tips, 1970. Bottom: Milk Tray, 1970s

Inspirations from cinema and television

The cinema has provided ad makers with a continuous stream of ideas across the decades. The film noir spoof *Dead Men Don't Wear Plaid* had US comedian Steve Martin interacting with characters from vintage 1930s and '40s movies – an idea that reappeared in the classic Holsten Pils campaign featuring British comic Griff Rhys Jones alongside Marilyn Monroe, John Wayne and other long-deceased Hollywood stars. Or think of the famous PG Tips 'Chimps' ads, which began life in 1956 after copywriter Rowley Marsh witnessed a chimps' tea party at London Zoo and whose most famous iteration took its inspiration from a Laurel and Hardy film. James Bond has inspired numerous campaigns, most famously the heavily 007-inflected 'And all because the lady loves...' series for Milk Tray. If, tonally, the latter campaign represents a fairly straight homage to the suave British spy, a growing sense of postmodernist mischief and subversion marked adaptations of cinematic ideas as the 1980s wore on. One particularly good example is the Carling Black Label spoof of the patriotic World War II-set film *The Dambusters*, in which a German soldier is seen diving like a goalkeeper to catch a British bomb. For the 2005 campaign to launch the new, updated version of

the classic Volkswagen GTI, the famous Gene Kelly street-dance sequence from the 1952 movie *Singin' in the Rain* was given a clever CGI makeover to endow Kelly's moves, and the accompanying soundtrack, with a distinctly contemporary feel – precisely what Volkswagen had done to its old GTI design, we were given to understand. The ad's tagline – 'The original, updated' – tidily expressed the process at work both in the creation of the ad and in the reworking of the product.

Television has also provided advertisers with plenty of inspiration. The journalistic practice of conducting 'vox pops' with members of the public for TV news segments was quickly adapted to its own ends by adland: passers-by were invited to take the 'Stork Challenge', which involved them trying to tell the difference between margarine and butter, from 1962 on. The popularity of soap operas and serials likewise led advertisers to create their own soap-style love sagas complete with cliffhangers, from the sixteen-year Cointreau campaign (from 1972) pairing the Anglo-French couple Catherine and Christian to the father-daughter twist of the Renault Clio 'Papa et Nicole' campaign (1991–98) and the Nescafé Gold Blend will they/won't they? couples of the late 1980s. The latter became something of a national obsession – to the point where the ads were the subject of an editorial in *The Times*. Crucially, the campaigns also helped boost sales of Gold Blend by 70 per cent, as well as spawning a top-ten CD of love songs (*Love over Gold*) and a bestselling novel.

Advertising has adopted a more irreverent tone since the 1980s, whether spoofing *The Dambusters* or updating Gene Kelly's dance moves. Opposite, top: Carling Black Label, 1989. Bottom: Volkswagen, 2005

The power of celebrity

Celebrities have regularly been enrolled to endorse products, of course, and not just ironically, as in the Heineken 'blackmail' campaign – although the twenty-first century is seeing more and more of this. Sometimes the connection between famous face and product is self-evident, as for instance when the globetrotting documentarist Alan Whicker was paired with Barclaycard in the 1980s to promote the idea of the universal acceptability of new-fangled credit cards. In the case of Brut's pre-metrosexual 'Splash It All Over' campaign in the 1970s, the endorsement of the boxer Henry Cooper was used to suggest that there was nothing wrong with real men wanting to smell nice. Advertisers usually want famous people to be themselves or, at least, to play up to their public image. In a neat twist on this convention, the famously likeable footballer Gary Lineker – sport's 'Mr Nice Guy' – has starred in a long-lasting campaign with Walkers Crisps in which he plays against type. Of course, the use of celebrity endorsements poses questions about their commitment to the product: do they *really* believe what, after all, they're usually being *paid* to say? This notion was tackled head-on in an ad for Egg financial services where one celebrity endorser was subjected to a lie-detector test at the hands of an FBI agent.

A beautiful mug.

www.NESCAFE.co.uk

NESCAFÉ®

Famous faces and popular new technologies have all been enrolled to help to sell products. Opposite, top: Walkers, 2010. This page, above: Nescafé, 2001. Left: Brut 33, 1970s. Bottom: Electricity Association, 1990s.

PUT A TIGER IN YOUR TANK!

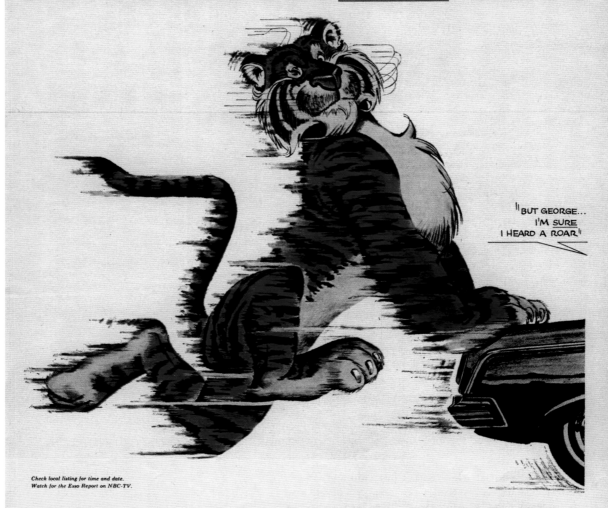

"BUT GEORGE...
I'M SURE
I HEARD A ROAR"

Check local listing for time and date.
Watch for the Esso Report on NBC-TV.

NEW POWER-FORMULA ESSO EXTRA GASOLINE BOOSTS POWER THREE WAYS:

1 **Cleaning Power!** Dirt can clog even a new carburetor in a few months of normal operation—causing hard starting and rough idling. Your very first tankful of New Esso Extra will start to clear away these deposits—in new engines or old—to improve power and mileage.

2 **Firing Power!** Spark plug and cylinder deposits can cause misfiring, pre-ignition and hot spots. New Esso Extra neutralizes these harmful deposits—to help your engine fire smoothly, to help preserve the power of new cars and restore lost power to many older cars.

3 **Octane Power!** New Esso Extra has the high octane that most cars now need for full smooth performance without knocking.
You'll get *all* these extras with New Power-formula Esso Extra gasoline—it puts a tiger in your tank! *Happy Motoring!*

HUMBLE
OIL & REFINING COMPANY

MAKERS OF FINE ESSO PRODUCTS
AND THE ESSO RACING FUELS THAT
POWERED A. J. FOYT AND RODGER

WARD TO FIRST AND SECOND PLACE
IN THIS YEAR'S INDIANAPOLIS 500
MEMORIAL DAY CLASSIC

ESSO

© HUMBLE OIL & REFINING COMPANY, 1964

Technological advances on both the big and small screens have been quickly taken up to bring novelty to campaigns, from the slow-motion replays borrowed from television sports coverage for the famous Tango 'Orange Man' campaign to the use of 'claymation', brought into vogue by Aardman's *Creature Comforts* short (1989), in Nick Park's ad for the Electricity Association (1990).

Maintaining brand loyalty

Consistency is a key part of building and maintaining brand loyalty; to this end, it's often one of the principal goals of an advertising campaign that it could potentially be sustained over many years. One famous adman listed his criteria for a good ad as follows: 'Did it make me gasp when I first saw it? Would I have liked to have thought of it myself? Is the idea unique? Does it fit the campaign strategy to perfection? Could it be used for up to 30 years?' Though longevity is a highly desirable attribute in advertising, freshness is no less crucial. Hence, although brand strategies might be retained across decades, they have to be reframed continually to respond to the zeitgeist. Knowing how to present an essentially unchanging product, and corporate identity, so that it appears constantly relevant to a changing society requires no little skill on the part of the advertising agency. Esso, for instance, began its long-standing relationship with the animal kingdom's symbol of power and energy, the tiger, in 1951, sparking a debate in parliament about whether the campaign encouraged dangerous driving. In 1964 the 'Put a Tiger in your Tank' slogan and cartoon tiger were unveiled, and in a neat marketing spin-off sticking a tiger tail on the back of your car suddenly became all the rage. When it was announced that Esso might then be getting rid of its tiger symbol, a national 'Save the Tiger' campaign was launched with widespread media coverage. As environmental concerns grew, the 'married and mortgaged' Esso tiger made his appearance, a family man with a family to look after.

Maintaining a consistent brand identity across advertising campaigns is one of the grails of good advertising. Esso certainly achieved longevity with its enduring tiger corporate symbol. Esso, 1960s

Katie says... OXO gives a meal man·appeal!

Some products have been strongly identified with flesh-and-blood symbols. Above: Oxo, 1950s. Opposite: Hathaway, 1960s

A lot of brands are associated with illustrated characters, from Kellogg's Snap, Crackle and Pop to Homepride's bowler-hatted 'flour men' and Tetley's flat-capped 'tea folk'. Other brands have developed identifiable flesh-and-blood symbols, an early and highly enigmatic, not to mention popular, example being Hathaway shirts' aristocrat with an eyepatch. From 1957 Oxo had a living, breathing character in the form of 'Katie', who used the famous little stock cube to deal with a series of kitchen dramas. Viewers identified with her: some wrote to her for advice, while female staff in one factory called a strike after an ad showed her husband speaking crossly to her. Feminism made the slogan associated with the early Katie ads – 'Oxo gives a meal man-appeal' – obsolete, while research carried out in the late 1970s suggested that Oxo's domestic goddess could sometimes make viewers feel a tad inadequate: cue the appearance of a more reassuringly realistic Oxo mum, with flaws for all to see.

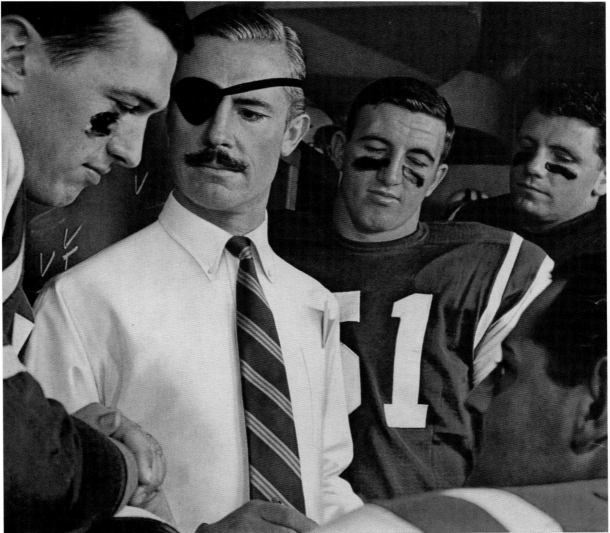

THE MAN, PHOTOGRAPHED WITH THE NEW YORK JETS. HIS SHIRT IS HATHAWAY'S NEW CLUB DRIP-DRY. IN YELLOW-JACKET AND 4 OTHER COLORS. ABOUT $9.00.

Hathaway's <u>yellow-jacket</u>: a subtle new color in a drip-dry Oxford cloth

—woven from an ingenious new blend of Dacron® and cotton

GOOD NEWS. Hathaway's canny weavers have just invented a refreshing new color *and* a remarkable new fabric. You see them both above.

The color is *yellow-jacket* — named after the small wasp of the same hue. Subtle, but with just enough dash to liven up your Fall wardrobe.

As for the fabric, it *looks* like traditional Oxford, *feels* like traditional

®DuPont registered trademark

Oxford — yet drip-dries overnight.

The clue to its performance is in the weaving—a totally new blend of 65 percent Dacron® polyester and 35 percent Oxford cotton.

Thanks to Dacron, this sumptuous stuff rarely needs ironing. And it stays crisp and unwilted through ball games, celebration parties and whatever.

Now turn your eye to the *cut* of the

cloth. Note the unobtrusive flare of the collar. And the trimness of the tapered body. Both are hallmarks of Hathaway's unique Club tailoring.

For this free *Dictionary of Shirts and Shirtings* and store names, write C. F. Hathaway, Dept. A-8, Waterville, Maine. In New York, call OXford 7-5566.

"Never wear a white shirt before sundown!" says Hathaway.
®

I dreamed I was a knockout
in my *maidenform* bra

Arabesque*...new Maidenform bra... has bias-cut center-of-attraction for *superb*
separation...insert of elastic for *comfort*...floral circular stitching for the most *beautiful* contours!

White in A, B, C cups, just 2.50. Also pre-shaped (light foam lining) 3.50.

Capturing the zeitgeist

Campaigns regularly tap into the zeitgeist. For instance, as women's liberation grew in importance in the 1970s and '80s, reversing gender roles became a popular strategy, as in this ad for 'Charlie', an early 'lifestyle' fragrance from Revlon. The popular 1988 'Changes' TV ad inverted some other gender stereotypes by having a woman (who was styled to look a bit like Princess Diana into the bargain) demonstrating a bit of girl power after a tearful break-up by getting into her beloved VW Golf and beginning to smile. 'If only everything in life was as reliable as a Volkswagen,' cooed the voiceover. The long-lasting 'Dream' campaign for Maidenform bras apparently had its origins in psychological research that pointed to women's exhibitionist tendencies. Early examples showed Maidenform Woman in a variety of scenarios in an exotic or otherwise unusual costume topped off with her (exposed) Maidenform bra. 'I dreamed I played Cleopatra in my Maidenform bra,' ran the text on one. 'I dreamed I was a knockout in my Maidenform bra,' ran another, its subject smiling beatifically in boxing gloves and satin shorts. A few decades later, in the age of gender equality, even Maidenform Woman dreamed herself into more businesslike settings, carrying a briefcase – but still with her bra exposed.

Shifting gender roles are clearly indicated in the different ways in which women have been portrayed in ads across the past half-century or so. Opposite: Maidenform, 1950s. This page, above left: Volkswagen Golf, 1988. Above right: Revlon Charlie, 1988

Would you be more careful if it was you that got pregnant?

It's a lot easier for a man to have a baby than for a woman.
She's the one who has to hump it around for nine months.
She's the one who has to grin and bear it. Backache,
morning sickness and all.
It's not a lot of fun being pregnant, if you don't want the
baby. It's not a lot of fun being an unwanted baby, either.

The Health Education Council

Anyone, married or single, can get advice on contraception, from their local family planning clinic.

Escaping the rational world

Since it aims to tap into people's deepest hopes and dreams, it's hardly surprising that advertising should regularly stray into the realm of the fantastical, venturing underwater or into the clouds, and the subtly (and not-so-subtly) sexual. The logic of the rational world has often been turned on its head in the promotion of good causes and utopian schemes, as in this iconic Saatchi & Saatchi poster for the Health Education Authority (shown left). And, of course, there's nothing ads enjoy more than challenging the stereotypes and conventions that advertising as an industry generally does so much to create in the first place.

Advertisers like to transport their target audiences into the clouds or beneath the waves, and they certainly don't have to obey the logic of the everyday world. Above: British Airways, 2005. Below: Health Education Authority, 1970s. Opposite, below: Rolex, 2005

Merry Christmas from **BRITISH AIRWAYS**

OYSTER PERPETUAL LADY-DATEJUST
PERFECTLY ACCESSORISED WITH PURPLE SEA FAN.

PROUD SPONSORS OF CORONATION STREET

Sex sells – as does challenging advertising conventions, as in this Dove campaign which rejoices in NOT using 'size 8 supermodels' to sell its products. Clockwise from above: Cadbury's Flake, 2006; Wall's Magnum, 2000s; Tom Ford, 2010; Dove, 2004

🐦 let's face it, firming the thighs of a size 8 supermodel is no challenge.

There's not much point in testing a new firming lotion on size-eight supermodel thighs, is there? That's why Dove's Firming range was tested on ordinary women with real lives to live – and real, curvy thighs to firm. After using Dove's nourishing and effective combination of moisturisers and seaweed extracts, we asked if they'd go in front of the camera. What better way to show the unretouched, unairbrushed results?

new Dove Firming Range

The shock of the new and the lure of nostalgia

Advertising is usually concerned with the new – edgy or cutting-edge youth-related phenomena, from street art to tattooing and body piercing, have regularly been co-opted to confer a little avant-garde cool on more traditional brands. Some of the most memorable ads, such as this one for the iPod, seem designed to make their products look like the very quintessence of modernity. But that hasn't stopped creatives from regularly deploying nostalgia – usually synonymous with the use of black-and-white photography – as a (hugely successful) selling tool: Ridley Scott's famous Hovis ad, conceived in the early 1970s at a time of massive national upheaval and social unrest, matched sepia-tinted footage with evocative music by Dvorak and a tagline of 'As good today as it's always been' (which, by the by, implies a great deal about the product's health-giving qualities without, usefully, making

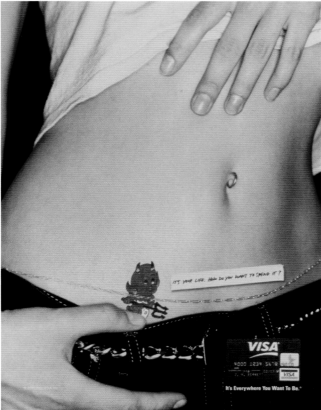

Some products are genuinely cutting-edge – the iPod, for instance – while adverts for other, more established ones try to borrow a little cutting-edge cool by associating themselves with youth movements. Above: iPod, 2004. Below: Visa, 2000s. Opposite: Maltesers, 2000s

any scientifically verifiable claims – see Principle 8) to great, and enduring, effect. When Boase Massimi Pollitt were asked to come up with a new campaign for Courage Best in the late 1970s, they suggested a humorously nostalgic, back-to-basics strategy emphasising the beer's traditional appeal. The resulting (highly popular) black-and-white TV ad was set in a Thirties-style pub with sawdust on the floor and drinkers in flat caps, and featured as its soundtrack an adapted version of a contemporary pop song, Chas 'n' Dave's 'Gertcha', with modified lyrics that expressed their disgust at modern drinking innovations ('Anything that comes with lemon in a slice – gertcha!'). Tony Kaye used a similar technique to quite different ends in his late 1980s 'Relax' ad for British Rail. The campaign drew angry complaints for its lack of realism – there was no mention of late trains or overcrowded carriages, for instance. Instead its sepia imagery, accompanied by a laidback bluegrass soundtrack, presented a languorously attractive vision of modern train travel.

Advertising is generally concerned with the new, but nostalgia remains a popular strategy with ad makers. Above: Hovis, 1970s. Opposite, top: Courage Best Beer, 1979. Bottom: British Rail, 1988

PRINCIPLE 6
THE MEDIUM IS – OR AT LEAST HAS A SERIOUS IMPACT ON – THE MESSAGE

PRINCIPLE 6
THE MEDIUM IS –
OR AT LEAST HAS
A SERIOUS IMPACT
ON – THE MESSAGE

Posters usually try to convey their messages in as few words as possible, but ads found on Tube platforms can afford to present their captive audiences with more text. *The Economist*, 2010

In advertising terms, it's probably not quite true to say, as sixties communications guru Marshall McLuhan suggested in his seminal study *Understanding Media: The Extensions of Man* (1964), that the medium is the message. All the same, the two elements are hard to separate, and it's certainly the case that no advertising message can be successfully delivered without careful attention first being paid to the particular qualities of the medium that is carrying it.

CHINA IS A FRIEND TO THE WEST

★ China makes a fifth of all the world's goods. It kits out the West's consumers and finances the West's borrowers.

★ China goes out of its way to emphasise that it wants a "peaceful rise". No other great power in history has done that.

★ China is the world's biggest investor in green technology.

WHERE DO YOU STAND?

For a free copy text PANDA to 60300.

Text messages to 60300 will be charged at your standard network rate. We will call or SMS you in order to get your delivery details and ask you whether you would like to receive other offers from The Economist. We will not use your mobile number for any other reason. UK residents only. One free copy per household.

BRITAIN SHOULD GIVE UP TRYING TO BE A GLOBAL POWER

▦ The rickety public finances mean we can no longer afford global ambitions: deep cuts to the defence budgets will seriously restrict our ability to fight wars abroad.

▦ It is foolish to resist the inevitable flow of power to emerging countries such as India and China. Our best course is to pool our influence and resources with other Europeans.

▦ Grandiose ambitions have led us into damaging misadventures, above all in Iraq, which have sapped trust in politics and demoralised the military.

WHERE DO YOU STAND?

For a free copy text GLOBAL to 60300.

Text messages to 60300 will be charged at your standard network rate. We will call or SMS you in order to get your delivery details and ask you whether you would like to receive other offers from The Economist. We will not use your mobile number for any other reason. UK residents only. One free copy per household.

Outdoor advertising doesn't have
to take the form of a conventional
poster, as this sculptural piece by
Clarity Coverdale Fury agency for
Clearway Minnesota

It is usually the advertising agency's media planning department that decides which media – from newspaper ads to more ambient forms – should be used in a given campaign in order to most effectively reach a target group of consumers. And since modern advertising campaigns regularly stretch across a variety of media, the campaign will have to be tweaked or recast for each medium. But whether it's a poster on the high street, an ad on TV or a banner on the web, the challenge of creating an ad that stands out from the crowd while being immediately comprehensible remains the same.

Outdoor advertising
Put simply, different media have different characteristics and so call for different kinds of creative approach. For instance, posters – or 'outdoor advertising' – have to be immediate in their impact if they are to grab the attention of busy passers-by. (It's no coincidence that, in the early days of road travel, billboards got bigger as cars got faster: the first full-colour billboard ad appeared in around 1925.) Town and city streets are full of visual clutter, so the simpler and bolder a poster is, the more likely it is to be successful. For the most part, both verbal and visual elements need to be punchy and to the point – although posters displayed on subway platforms, for instance, can afford to be more discursive since travellers spend on average three minutes waiting for their train and have limited options as to how they are going to pass that time. Ads of this sort come in various shapes and sizes – from fly posters all the way up to 32-, 48- and even 96-sheet billboard posters – and have on occasion featured enterprising 3D additions, as in the hoarding for Araldite glue which featured an actual Ford Cortina or the Indian 'clothesline' billboard ad for Ariel shown on the following pages.

Three-dimensional elements can really make an advert stand out from the crowd. Ariel, 2003. Araldite, 1990s

Enjoying the rare luxury of being unconstrained by precise spatial templates into which their work must fit, advertisers have come up with some brilliantly imaginative solutions. Though one of the attractions of poster campaigns is their high public visibility, it's nonetheless possible – and, indeed, essential – to secure the most appropriate sites for them to be displayed. For certain products, that might mean close to a point of sale, or it might mean at a location where the target consumer group might be expected to gather – an airport, for instance.

Newspapers and magazines

By contrast, press ads – that is, ads that appear in newspapers and magazines – have something of a captive audience and so can afford to draw readers in more gradually. That audience, of course, will usually be much more precisely defined than is the case with a poster campaign: most publications have well-defined readerships with proven interests and a clear socioeconomic profile, factors that the agency's media planners will have taken into account when booking space in a particular publication in the first place. Though expansive verbal content is becoming less fashionable, particularly as global brands look to create image-led campaigns that transcend linguistic barriers, creating space for discursive copy has its advantages, allowing advertisers to shape longer 'stories' and include a lot more detail about their products. Other traditional ways to connect with a target group, such as free samples, brochures and direct-mail inserts, can also be included in magazines.

One key feature that all such 'static' ads share – whether poster or press ad – is the relationship between words and image. In the best examples of both, as mentioned above, the copy should never be merely a caption for the image, nor should the image simply illustrate what the text says. The best advertising practitioners are able to have fun with the space between the two elements, using it to create the grail of all ad creatives – surprise.

Advertising that eschews traditional formats stands a good chance of capturing the attention of passers-by, as with this eye-catching piece of guerrilla advertising for *The Sopranos*. Opposite: Planet M, 2001

Television and cinema

TV ads have potentially many more elements, not least spoken dialogue and music. The first television advertisement – for Bulova watches – was broadcast in the USA on 1 July 1941. It cost $9, lasted for twenty seconds and featured an image of a clock superimposed on a map of the United States, with a voiceover that announced 'America runs on Bulova time'. The famously long-running Benson & Hedges 'Happiness Is...' campaign was the first to use music as an integral part of the product's identity: Bach's 'Air on a G String' became more or less synonymous with the cigar brand. Historically TV ads have both reached the biggest audiences and most closely approximated 'art': after all, the resources available to TV ad makers are essentially the same as those available to the great cinematic auteurs. Given this symbiotic relationship, it's perhaps unsurprising that cinema has provided so much inspiration to ad makers over the years, and likewise that a number of celebrated ad makers have also had careers as filmmakers, Ridley Scott (*Alien, Gladiator*), Alan Parker (*Bugsy Malone, Fame*) and Hugh Hudson (*Chariots of Fire*) being notable examples. If the first TV ads were essentially brief illustrated lectures featuring a presenter talking to camera, they soon developed the full armoury of cinematic techniques, with ad makers sometimes going to extraordinary lengths to tell their 30- or 40-second stories as dynamically as they could. Scott started out making ads in a basement studio on Wardour Street in London's Soho, but his ambition was always to emulate the cinematic greats. 'I would take Orson Welles as my inspiration for lighting a soap powder ad in a kitchen,' he once said. He based one ad for toothpaste on David Lean's classic screen adaptation of *Dr Zhivago*.

Guerrilla advertising uses
unconventional means to capture
people's attention, as with these
campaigns for plastic surgery
and Playboy

Brief
During the summer the Playboy Magazine looked for a Playmate among the girls on the beach. To do this they organised a competition with a jury which had to select a future covergirl for this prestigious magazine.

Idea
To encourage the girls to participate in the competition they decided to give them each a beach mat where the girls could lie and sunbathe as though they were on the front page of the magazine.

The proliferation of channels means that it's hard now to achieve the kind of viewer figures that were possible in the 1970s, but the fragmentation of the TV audience does allow for better targeting of a particular demographic or consumer group. Cinema ads enjoy identical resources, but can perhaps afford to adopt a more playful tone since they have a captive, and often more receptive, audience – cinema audiences are there to be entertained and anyway don't have the option of walking out to put the kettle on when the ads start.

Guerrilla and non-traditional advertising

All advertising is designed to create a 'buzz' of some sort. In recent decades, non-traditional methods have increasingly been incorporated into multimedia campaigns to achieve this effect. Such innovative methods include so-called 'ambient media', which range from carrier bags and logos on clothing to beach mats, drinking cups and an arm hanging from the boot of a New York taxi. This kind of guerrilla advertising is intended to catch consumers off-guard and get under their radars. One particularly intriguing type of such guerrilla campaigns is so-called viral advertising, which involves potential consumers passing on material to one another via email and so draws them into participating in the promotion of the product in question. One of the most successful viral campaigns to date helped launch the hugely successful indie horror film *The Blair Witch Project* (1999), which went on to achieve an extraordinarily high profit-to-cost ratio: it's been calculated that, for every dollar spent on making and promoting it, the movie grossed more than $10,000. A website launched a year before the film was released aimed to create an 'urban myth' that the events portrayed in the movie were true and that the film was a documentary rather than a dramatic construct. Hype grew, and fake 'missing persons' leaflets for the trio

The Blair Witch Project **exploited the new medium of the internet to extraordinary effect. Given how cluttered the web has since become, can its success ever be replicated?**

of filmmakers were distributed on US college campuses. Of course, the campaign dates from the early days of web uptake, when there was less competition for attention and a much greater sense of novelty. It's questionable whether the *Blair Witch* phenomenon could ever be replicated.

Indeed, these days the internet is as cluttered as the streets of any great metropolis – the web is a vast growth area for advertising spending, which is estimated to have increased globally from $9 billion in 2002 to $70 billion at the beginning of this decade – so an effective online ad has to be as at least as good at rising above the competing visual din as a traditional 96-sheet poster intended for display on a city-centre billboard. Though the quality of the image seen by the end user is harder to control (being dependent on such things as quality of internet connection and screen resolution), there are nonetheless many attractive aspects to online advertising – it's global in its reach, available 24/7 and particularly appealing to a young, techno-savvy audience. (Some might say that it's equally appealing to the older, time- and money-rich 'silver surfer' generation, though this market has been less well exploited.)

The internet revolution

Which brings us squarely to a subject that has revolutionised the advertising industry – in common with most other areas of human endeavour – over the past decade: the internet. Dan Douglass, Executive Creative Director at London-based agency MRM Meteorite, assesses the changes wrought by the new digital era as follows: 'I've been in advertising for twenty-six years, and I could never have imagined that it would go down to the level of the individual so much in terms of the individual consumer having far more power and influence. The traditional models according to which all marketers operated

In October of 1994
three student filmmakers disappeared
in the woods near Burkittsville, Maryland
while shooting a documentary...

A year later their footage was found.

THE BLAIR WITCH PROJECT

ARTISAN ENTERTAINMENT PRESENTS A HAXAN FILMS PRODUCTION HEATHER DONAHUE   MICHAEL WILLIAMS   JOSHUA LEONARD "THE BLAIR WITCH PROJECT"
PRODUCTION DESIGNER BEN ROCK   ART DIRECTOR RICARDO R. MORENO   DIRECTOR OF PHOTOGRAPHY NEAL FREDERICKS   MUSIC BY ANTONIO CORA   EXECUTIVE PRODUCED BY BOB EICK AND KEVIN J. FOXE
CO-PRODUCED BY MICHAEL MONELLO   PRODUCED BY GREGG HALE & ROBIN COWIE   WRITTEN, DIRECTED AND EDITED BY DANIEL MYRICK & EDUARDO SANCHEZ

COMPANION ALBUM
AVAILABLE ON

www.blairwitch.com

ARTISAN

have been turned on their heads. You can no longer go out with a big brand campaign and expect to increase your brand equity overnight because people are Tweeting and are on Facebook, talking about your campaign in a way that fundamentally affects your brand equity. Consequently clients have to be far more multidimensional about the way they plan their media and their communication campaign.'

Viral successes have become something of a holy grail among marketers, but the process is unpredictable. 'You can't account for the fact that content online will go viral,' warns Douglass. 'A lot of people talk about viral as if it's a medium. It isn't: you create content that goes viral and there's absolutely no way of knowing what's going to go viral. That's what's changed. The science of advertising – the traditional awareness models, prompted/unprompted, the means by which the success of campaigns were gauged – has become even more uncertain, because the reins of control are far more in the hands of the customer or consumer. They have the immediate power to feed back and change the course of your approach.' Viral marketing may be an unpredictable business, but when advertisers get it right, it does work: MRM Meteorite's own 'Giant Jar' viral film helped draw an extra 100,000 visitors to the Argos website and generate over £3.6 million in incremental revenue for the retailer.

The growth in digital 'people power' presents new opportunities for businesses, something that advertising agencies are increasingly exploiting on their clients' behalf. Says Douglass: 'We have a very strong data planning department at MRM Meteorite. We take the raw data from clients, segment it and then target consumers by segment with messages that are relevant, timely and resonant to those particular groups. Data is real-time now in the digital world. You need that feedback loop to be instant to have any effect on your consumer.' He offers an example of the online version of the age-old marketers' favourite, direct mailing: 'We run the

Any space can potentially be turned into an advertising site, as with the brilliant, multi-award-winning 'Life's Too Short' campaign for a German online recruitment website. Jobsintown.de, 2000s

Viral ads are unpredictable, but can be hugely successful in engaging audiences in new and surprising ways, as with MRM Meteorite's 'Giant Jar' film for Argos, 2007

The internet is increasingly the place we go to in order to do our shopping, but do successful sites still need TV advertising to help promote their services? Web phenomenon Gumtree aired its first TV ad in 2010

Costa Coffee loyalty programme in the UK and we came up with the Costa Coffee card. That's been a tremendous success. There are 2.5 million active cardholders. You go into Costa, your card is swiped, we know your likes and preferences. We send you an email with your points tally and serve up suggestions as to how to use those points. We can get a lot clearer and tighter now on customer behaviour: where they're spending, how they're spending, the propensity to buy food as well as coffee, it's all far more granular than it was before. And people are happy to express what they want because they get something back. It's about an exchange. That's really what we do [as an agency]: we give customers reasons to interact, to continue to interact.'

As a result of the growing importance of online communications, agencies have to be technically capable, and more. 'If you're reliant on the technology to deliver, you have to make absolutely sure it's capable of doing it because one bad experience can really affect your relationship with your customers. So you have to make sure that the way the whole thing is delivered online is really watertight. That represents a real investment. But let's be in no doubt that it's all valueless without a big idea. You can invest hundreds of millions of pounds on the technology side but you still need

strong, resonant, relevant, powerful and differentiating ideas. That hasn't changed. To that extent we are still Mad Men. A big idea is an organising thought, something around which everything can revolve creatively. We can get carried away with technology, with delivery, with this notion of digital. For me, digital is a broader canvas on which you can play out a big idea, but it's still in need of a big idea, a central co-ordinating creative thought, and that will never go away.'

Mike Widdis concurs on the last point, and adds some caveats with regard to digital as a domain for wide-reaching campaigns: 'The amount of money spent on online advertising is huge and growing exponentially. But digital is very fragmented. You can measure website hits but that doesn't necessarily translate into purchases. Online works but it works 150 per cent better if it has offline support. Accountability is why clients love it. If I spend £1 million on television advertising across a weekend, nobody knows for sure what's happened as a result, whereas with digital advertising the effect is more measurable.' He concludes: 'The business is moving faster all the time, with results being monitored and fed back into the system at an increasing rate, but people's underlying attitudes change more slowly.' And in many cases, of course, it is precisely those underlying attitudes that advertisers are trying to influence.

PRINCIPLE 7
THERE'S NO SUCH THING AS BAD PUBLICITY

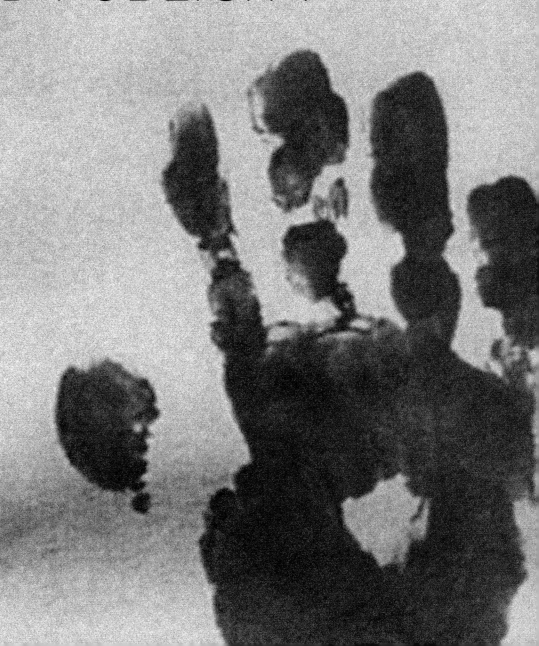

PRINCIPLE 7
THERE'S NO SUCH THING AS BAD PUBLICITY

When the Wonderbra 'Hello Boys' campaign was launched on huge billboards across the UK on 14 February 1994, road-safety experts expressed a fear that the image of Eva Herzigova in her underwear might cause some drivers to become distracted, while some women's groups complained that the image was exploitative. The result? Oceans of free press coverage and soaring sales for Wonderbra.

Advertising is expensive: in addition to the cost of creating the ad in the first place, there's then the cost of buying space – whether for a print ad on the back page or inside front cover of a prestigious glossy magazine or a slot for a 30-second mini-epic on prime-time telly – so that it can actually be seen by its target audience. So it's always very welcome when ads generate further unpaid coverage for themselves in the media by becoming 'stories' in their own right. Controversy and disapproval (so long as it's not expressed by the target audience) can be useful selling tools, and may even help to strengthen brand loyalty by making consumers feel, as one commentator has put it, like members of 'a slightly rebellious club'.

Creating media hype

Sometimes, generating free media hype seems to be the principal driving force behind a campaign. For instance, in the late 1990s pet-food manufacturer Whiskas produced a revolutionary ad that was purportedly aimed at cats rather than their owners. And Ketchum Life, the agency responsible for the campaign, went to some trouble to produce an ad that would appeal to them, using Pedigree's pet nutrition research centre to discover the colours, noises and movements that cats respond to and then featuring them prominently in the ad itself, which was aired on prime-time ITV. To maximise the impact of the campaign and make sure it received as much attention as possible, the agency produced a teaser campaign

This ad for Whiskas cat food was designed to appeal directly to cats rather than their owners. Because this strategy was so unusual, it also generated a lot of (free) comment in the media

which involved sending bowls bearing the words 'the most exciting night of your nine lives' to known cat-enthusiast journalists in advance of the ad's first broadcast. Numerous British newspapers, including such mass-circulation titles as *The Sun*, *The Times* and the *London Evening Standard*, picked up on the story. A VNR (video news release), a faux-news report on the campaign featuring an animal behaviourist and footage of cats watching the ad as well as clips of old Whiskas commercials, helped to secure coverage on other television networks including Channel 5, Sky and even the non-commercial BBC. In fact, the story went global, with broadcasters in France, Canada and the US also paying attention. In some ways this was a campaign that, in aiming its 'message' at cats themselves, flouted one of the cardinal rules of advertising – target the purchaser. But at the same time, by cannily making the most of its own novelty value, it achieved huge across-the-board attention beyond what might otherwise have been possible on a comparatively modest budget. In 2011, Nestlé repeated the trick by producing an ad for its Purina dog food in Austria that featured high-frequency sounds designed to cause canines to jump up and down so that their owners would be encouraged to buy Purina rather than competing brands whose ads failed to provoke a similarly Pavlovian reaction in their pets.

Provoking controversy

Another cardinal rule of advertising was broken by the 'United Colors' campaign run by the global fashion brand Benetton. This featured a series of shockingly graphic and/or provocative images – an AIDS sufferer on his deathbed; a black horse mating with a white one – that bore no obvious relation to any products sold by the company. The 1991 image of a newborn child, unwashed and with its umbilical cord still attached, found its way into *Guinness World Records* in 2000 as the 'most controversial campaign' ever; certainly a large number of complaints were made to the British Advertising Standards Authority. 'We don't imagine that we are able to resolve human problems, but nor do we want to pretend that they don't exist.

UNITED COLORS
OF BENETTON.

We believe advertising can be used to say something besides selling a product – something more useful,' said the architect of the company's approach, photographer Oliviero Toscani. 'Why is traditional advertising acceptable with its fake images, yet reality is not?' he argued on another occasion. 'We think we have a duty to talk about such things.' Was the principal aim of Benetton's campaign really to bring taboo subjects into the open, or just to invite media controversy? One thing is for sure: as a strategy, it generated a huge amount of media coverage and significantly increased brand awareness. The company repeated the trick at the end of 2011 when it launched its 'Unhate' campaign, which showed leaders from opposite sides of the political and religious spectrum apparently kissing one another. In an example of guerrilla advertising, an image of the pope seemingly kissing an Egyptian imam was draped over a bridge near the Vatican, which responded with dismay. Alessandro Benetton defended the campaign by saying it was designed to give publicity to 'an ideal notion of tolerance'.

With its 'United Colors' campaign, Benetton helped launch a whole new genre: shock advertising or 'shockvertising'. Employing provocative imagery and tapping into taboo areas has since become a common strategy for gaining attention, as in this Indian ad for hand gel. On the whole, though, clients with products and services to sell, and strong corporate images to protect, rarely agree to underwrite disturbing or

With its 'United Colors' campaign, Benetton helped to launch the idea of 'shockvertising' – using any visual means available, no matter how shocking, to get your message across. Benetton, 1996. Benetton, 2011

Public-health and charity advertising campaigns regularly opt to deliver their messages with maximum force – shock is part of their message. More unusual is the daring Indian ad for Sanitol hand gel shown here. Opposite, top: PETA, 1990s; Deutscher Tierschutzbund, 2010

hard-hitting campaigns, no matter how attention-grabbing they might prove to be. By contrast, charities and other such bodies regularly agree to the use of shock tactics in order to put their messages over as powerfully as possible. Uncomfortable visual material is perhaps unavoidable when tackling issues such as child suffering or drug abuse. Of course, there is always a danger that it will put the target audience off – the old adage 'there's no such thing as bad publicity' isn't beyond challenge even in the context of public health campaigns. After receiving a large number of complaints, the Advertising Standards Authority censured the posters in the National Health 'Get Unhooked' anti-smoking campaign for being likely to frighten and distress children. Did these ads go too far, or was the graphic nature of the campaign justified?

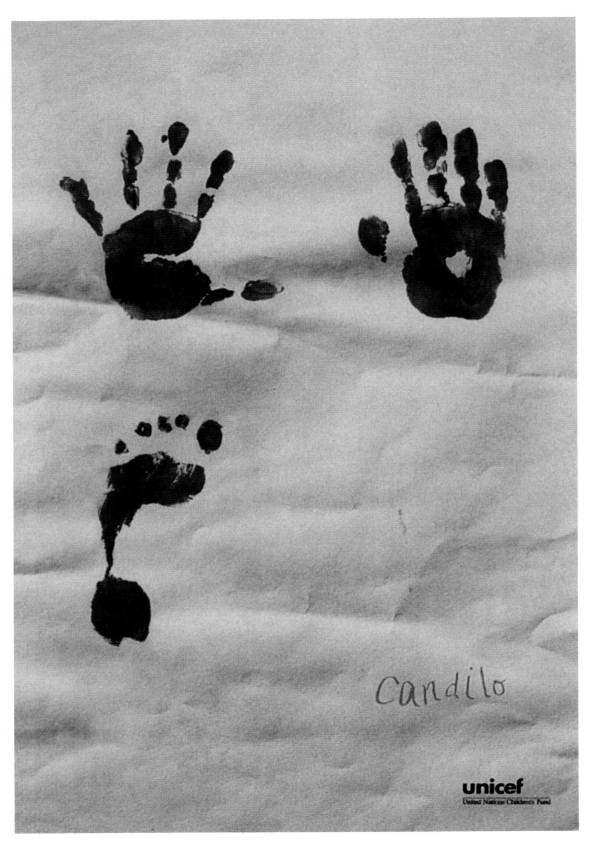

Candilo

unicef
United Nations Children's Fund

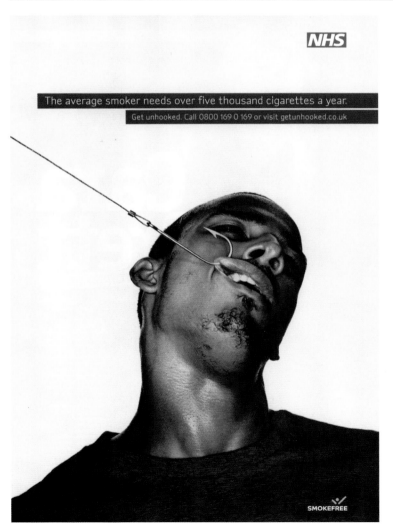

Sharing your mate's works means sharing with everyone he's ever shared with.

Shooting up once can screw you up. Forever.

NHS

The average smoker needs over five thousand cigarettes a year.

Get unhooked. Call 0800 169 0 169 or visit getunhooked.co.uk

SMOKEFREE

Important messages need to be delivered with maximum force to rise above the visual din of other advertising. But is there a risk that shocking images will put some people off? This page, top: Central Office of Information, 1989. Bottom: NHS, 2006. Opposite: Unicef, 2003

PRINCIPLE 8
RESTRICTIONS WILL SET YOU FREE

PRINCIPLE 8
RESTRICTIONS WILL SET YOU FREE

Surrealism is part of the language of modern advertising, from hairy snooker balls to fish riding bicycles. Kaminomoto, 1990s. Guinness, 1996

There are various laws and standards that advertisers have to comply with when they are planning a media campaign. In the UK, regulation is handled by the Advertising Standards Authority (ASA), which enforces codes that cover everything from traditional print-based ads to commercial emails and SMS text-message ads. In the US it is the Federal Trade Commission, and similar bodies exist in other countries. If you're advertising internationally, you need to be aware of variations between territories.

Be careful of what you promise
Products that are particularly tightly regulated in this respect include the obvious – alcohol, cigarettes – but there are also guidelines that relate more generally to 'truth claims'. Ads generally promise to make consumers' lives better in some way or other, but how they do so is carefully monitored by regulators. In this regard, the lessons Lord Peter Wimsey learned during his brief tenure at Pym's in the early 1930s – where he discovered that 'any advertisements containing the word "cure", though there was no objection to such expressions as "relieve"

You seem above the problems of the world with a glass of Double Diamond. There's nothing like this full-bodied Burton beer for putting fresh heart into you. A Double Diamond never lets you down—it's always as enjoyable as it was the last time. Drop in for a Double Diamond tonight.

A DOUBLE DIAMOND
works wonders

IND COOPE'S **DOUBLE DIAMOND** BREWED AT BURTON

7mg TAR 0·7mg NICOTINE
SMOKING CAUSES HEART DISEASE
Health Departments' Chief Medical Officers

Alcohol and cigarette advertising has been an area of particular visual innovation – perhaps as a direct result of the restrictions imposed on ad makers by regulatory bodies. Above: Silk Cut, 1980s. Opposite: Double Diamond, 1950s

or "ameliorate"', might find themselves under challenge – haven't changed that much. Standards do continue to evolve, however: what might have been acceptable in 1956 – such as the innocent-sounding slogan 'Don't forget the Fruit Gums, Mum' – might not pass muster today (playing on 'pester power' is discouraged in relation to products aimed at children).

Challenging the imagination

Fortunately, tighter regulation does not necessarily mean less imaginative advertising. Quite the opposite, in fact. For instance, expat British adman Neil French has said that he has a particular fondness for his inventive 1991 ads for Japanese hair tonic Kaminomoto – the example shown on the previous spread plays on the phrase 'as bald as a billiard ball' – precisely because of the restrictions he faced in the particular Asian market for which they were created. 'I like them because the Singapore government makes it impossible to advertise Kaminomoto,' he said. 'You couldn't show the product. You couldn't show pictures of bald men. These ads are an exaggeration – hair on an egg, hair on billiard balls – which is what advertising is always about.' That exaggeration is made particularly appealing here by the winking understatement of the copy, which visually is reduced to the status of a footnote: 'Be careful with the Kaminomoto.' The campaign is said to have boosted sales of the product by 1,000 per cent.

The standards governing alcohol advertising were looser when the London agency S.H. Benson came up with the slogan 'Guinness is good for you' in 1929. But regulations disallowing the suggestion that drinking alcohol improves performance or health or leads to social or professional success pushed creatives to explore more freewheeling, off-the-wall ideas over the following decades. The slogan 'Guinnless isn't good for you' wittily echoed the earlier campaign, while Tony Kaye's 1996 'A Woman Needs a Man Like a Fish Needs a Bicycle' ad for the drink lifted off into altogether more surreal territory,

Heineken refreshes the parts other beers cannot reach.

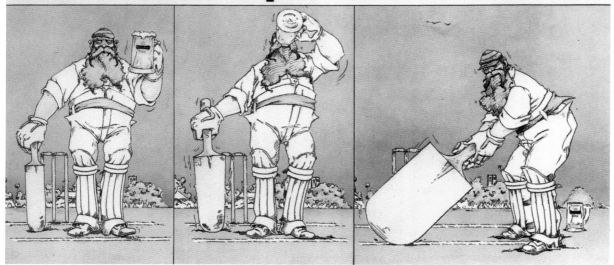

Cricket and ancient Egypt are not the first things that come to mind when you think about beer and cigarettes. Is that partly why these campaigns have proved so memorable? Above: Heineken, 1970s. Opposite: Benson and Hedges, 1980s. Benson and Hedges, 1977

showing a series of images of women doing jobs traditionally associated with men before ending with footage showing a fish riding a bicycle. This last image became a hugely popular screensaver. Indeed, many of the most memorable campaigns and slogans of the past half-century or so have come from brewers showing off the transformatory powers of their products while avoiding making claims that are overly specific about their practical effects.

Of course, ethics in advertising isn't only a question for regulatory bodies. Occasionally ad agencies themselves have taken moral stands: for instance, as health fears relating to smoking gathered force in the 1960s, Ogilvy and Mather and Doyle Dane Bernbach both declared that they would not accept business from cigarette manufacturers. Nonetheless, ethical issues aside, prior to the imposition of a complete ban on all such activities in Britain in 1999, cigarette advertising was a site of significant visual innovation, with ever tighter regulations necessitating increasingly imaginative, allusive creative solutions, culminating in the Benson and Hedges 'Surreal' campaign, which turned most of the rules of advertising on their head by eschewing text (statutory health warning aside) and requiring its visually literate audience actively to seek out the product in the picture.

PRINCIPLE 9
ONCE IS NEVER ENOUGH

PRINCIPLE 9
ONCE IS NEVER ENOUGH

The exception that proves the rule: Apple's '1984' ad was only screened nationally once but generated a huge response. Most other advertisers have to pay to have their message repeated many times to achieve a similar impact

In advertising, once is never enough – repetition is key to getting your message across. According to one advertising professional, the attitude prior to the 1960s 'Creative Revolution' was: 'It doesn't really matter what you're saying just as long as you keep saying it.' Though the manner in which advertisers 'said' things changed dramatically thereafter, with subtler, more allusive strategies being adopted, the idea that ubiquity is key to permeating consumers' consciousnesses remained – and remains – uncontested. However you frame and encode your message, unless people get the chance to see it, it will inevitably fail to communicate itself effectively.

On January 24th,
Apple Computer will introduce
Macintosh.
And you'll see why 1984
won't be like "1984".

A cuppa's much nicer with a Kit Kat. So is school milk. So's a football match, television, the office coffee-break. Every time your family has a break, a Kit Kat would make it nicer. Get some today— and have them ready.

Have a break—have a Kit Kat

Repetition remains one of the essential elements of advertising – which means repeating the same ad in different places and at different times, and maintaining a consistent brand identity across many years, as with these ads for Kit-Kat from the 1960s and the present century

In the digital age, advertising operates in an increasingly diversified and fragmented marketplace; it's therefore essential to secure optimum visibility for your ad. That's a process that begins when you choose the publication or website where you intend to advertise, of course. But there is a further stage, which is ensuring that you achieve maximum visibility within that publication, etc. Where your advertisement appears on the page will have an effect on response levels. Top-half or outside-edge positions generally perform best.

Frequency is key... unless you're Apple

Purchasing space can be the most expensive part of the advertising process, but skimping on repeat advertising is rarely wise. Frequency is essential to giving an advert a chance of working. Planning a campaign means setting a budget. Knowing how much to spend is never easy: a rule of thumb for large companies might be 5 per cent of annual turnover, but the amounts will be considerably higher for companies at launch stage. Some so-called 'category-killer' campaigns are designed to ensure that an established leading brand maintains its market dominance purely through its advertising presence: smaller, would-be challenger brands are discouraged from competing simply because they are unable to match the leader's advertising budget. A consistent advertising presence lodges the brand's name in people's minds, whereas a parsimonious approach to spending will often fail to create such familiarity. Success in advertising is not for the financially faint-hearted.

Of course, every rule has its exception. Apple Computers' much-acclaimed '1984' television ad – which introduced the mass US viewing public to the Mac – was aired nationally only once, on 22 January 1984, in the middle of Super Bowl XVIII. The epic 60-second ad, directed by Ridley Scott, showed a female athlete escaping the clutches of Orwellian thought police and running towards a screen bearing the image of a Big Brother-figure, at which she hurls a sledgehammer. This highly enigmatic piece of image making was conceived as a

piece of 'event' TV, appropriately introducing a product that would do nothing less than help reshape global culture in the coming decades to the largest annual television audience in the USA. Though Apple only paid to have the advert screened nationally once, its impact was such that it was rebroadcast and discussed at length on news and analysis programmes the same night. Its absence from the commercials slots thereafter only added to its mystique so that it developed an enigmatic allure. Hence, Apple's failure to pay for the ad to be aired regularly certainly didn't stop people talking about it. It won the 'Grand Prix' at that year's prestigious Cannes Lions International Advertising Festival, and has since come top of numerous 'greatest commercial of all time' polls. Not bad for an ad that was shown commercially on national television only once, but on this occasion it was its scarcity value – its boldness in the face of the 'once is never enough' rule – that secured the ad so much attention. Which brings us neatly to our final Principle of Advertising...

PRINCIPLE 10
IGNORE ALL RULES AND PRESCRIPTIONS

PRINCIPLE 10
IGNORE ALL RULES
AND PRESCRIPTIONS

Every great ad man or woman will tell you that rule-breaking is at the heart of the advertiser's art. In one scene in *Mad Men*, leading Fifth Avenue creative Don Draper shakes his head in disbelief over a black-and-white magazine ad for Volkswagen cars. Lots of real advertising people shared the fictional Draper's bemusement when Doyle Dane Bernbach's now-iconic series of ads which urged consumers to 'think small' and the like began to appear in the 1960s. They seemed to go against every principle of advertising – and yet they worked.

> A poster should contain no more than eight words, which is the maximum the average reader can take in at a single glance. This, however, is a poster for Economist readers.

**Rules are there to be broken.
The *Economist* ad shown above
even explains its own rule-breaking.
Opposite: Smirnoff, 1999**

The writings of David Ogilvy, not least his bestselling *Confessions of an Advertising Man*, are full of rules: 'when your advertisement is to contain a coupon and you want the maximum returns, put it at the top, bang in the middle', etc. But he nonetheless created a business that broke all the rules. Advertising is all about connecting with your target audience, and sometimes the best way of doing that is to turn convention on its head. For instance, research has regularly suggested that colourless (and therefore characterless) bottles are a drawback in advertising terms, but they've been at the heart of some of the most imaginative campaigns of recent times.

Copywriter Ed McCabe said: 'I have no use for rules. They only rule out the brilliant exception.' The great Bill Bernbach was always keen to remind his peers that advertising is essentially an art – the art of persuasion – rather than a strict science. 'Rules are what the artist breaks,' he once noted; 'the memorable never emerged from a formula.'

Remember: doing it all the 'wrong' way – going against received wisdom at every turn – is sometimes the only way to get things absolutely 'right'. That could even be one of the 10 Principles of Advertising.

CHECKLISTS

CHECKLISTS

INTRODUCTION

1. Arm yourself with a notebook. As many of the examples contained in this book show, you never know where and when you will find good ideas for future campaigns. Make sure you're in a position to make a note of it when inspiration does strike.

2. Get into the habit of looking at as many ads as possible – you need to know what other advertisers are doing.

3. When you see a particularly good ad, try to define what you find particularly successful about it. Keep examples of striking fonts, colours, types of imagery, word play etc.

4. Be especially aware of ads that capture your attention when you're focusing on something else. How do they do that? The modern world is full of ads – the ability to make people take notice of yours amidst all the visual clutter is invaluable.

5. To be successful in advertising, you need to be able to see the bigger picture. Make sure you read newspapers, including the financial pages, so that you can understand marketing and advertising questions from all perspectives.

PRINCIPLE 1:
KNOW YOUR AUDIENCE

1. Who are your target consumers?

2. Gather as much factual information about them (e.g. age range, sex, average income) as you can.

3. Can you evoke this group through other things that might link them – the kind of television programmes or music they might be interested in, or the kind of language they use and that sets them apart from other social groups (e.g. the way teenagers speak as compared with their parents)?

4. If the product you are creating an ad for is already available to buy, find out what the target group thinks about it. How is it differentiated in their eyes from competing brands? If it is brand-new, research rival or associated products.

5. Write a brief based on the answers to the questions above, describing your target audience and their perceptions of your product or service and drawing attention to anything you think might be useful in a creative context.

6. Has anything you have learned from talking to your target audience suggested that there may be a related product that could usefully be developed? Is the manufacturer missing an interesting opportunity in the marketplace?

PRINCIPLE 2:
BEHIND EVERY GREAT ADVERTISING CAMPAIGN IS A GREAT CREATIVE CONCEPT

1. Read the brief generated by the questions under Principle 1, then do as much independent research as possible into your product. Afterwards, list ALL the possible benefits associated with your product. Consumers generally buy things when they think they will make their lives better.

2. What parts of the description of the target audience generated by Principle 1 might be useful in creating an ad, e.g. language used, shared interests?

3. At this point it's time to narrow down your product benefits to settle on a USP/ ESP. Focusing on that, produce as many 'creative concepts' as you can. You can never have too many good ideas.

4. Carry out an 'overnight test' on your initial concepts. Which looks best the following morning? Make a rough sketch of it.

5. Carry out a 'SIMPLES' analysis of the sketch. Does it meet all the criteria?

PRINCIPLE 3:
LESS IS MORE

1. How is your product different from rival brands? How can that difference be underlined in terms of the way your ad 'positions' it?

2. Look at the way the idea of 'creaminess' was exploited in the Boddingtons campaign. Find an adjective that captures the essence of your product and then come up with a series of associated words or images. Could one of these more lateral ideas form the basis of a campaign for your product?

3. Write a catchphrase/slogan for your product. Make sure the language is appropriate to the target audience.

4. If you are creating an ad for TV, radio or another appropriate medium, produce a jingle for it. Think about mood as well as the words: are they both likely to appeal to your target audience?

5. Look again at the ideas you have generated so far. How complicated would they be to realise in practical terms? Look more closely at the most ambitious idea you have produced so far. Is the message you are trying to deliver still easy to understand?

PRINCIPLE 4:
A PICTURE IS WORTH A THOUSAND WORDS – BUT NEVER UNDER-ESTIMATE THE POWER OF A GREAT HEADLINE

1. Whatever medium you are working in, your ad will almost certainly contain a mixture of words and images. Do they duplicate or repeat one another in any way? If they do, try to reduce any areas of overlap. Ads should be as economical in their expression as possible.

2. Ads that set a little puzzle are often more successful in getting viewers' attention than ads that are too obvious. Does your ad force viewers to work something out or to make a connection for themselves?

3. Look again at the visual elements in your ad. Are they surprising in some way? If they lack surprise, can you think of a way to make them more attention-grabbing or unusual? Avoid producing visual muzak at all costs.

4. How do the words/images appeal particularly to your target group of consumers? If the ad is humorous, is it funny in a way that will appeal to them particularly? Try to get into the mind of your ideal audience.

5. How is the font or setting of the text appropriate to your product and audience? If you're unsure, look at the sorts of magazines, etc that your target viewers usually read.

6. Step away from your ad. When you return to it, try to map how a viewer's eye will travel around it. In terms of the balance between different elements and their placement in the ad, does it begin and end where it should? Does it tell a coherent 'story'?

7. Does the ad contain all the crucial practical information – for instance, a website address – that it needs to?

PRINCIPLE 5:
ORIGINALITY IS JUST COPYING WITH A TWIST

1. Would a 'scientific' or market research-based presentation be appropriate to your product? Try to write an ad based on one of the classic 'scientific' formulas.

2. Try to define your ad in terms of how it makes its appeal to viewers: is it humorous, sentimental, class-based, nostalgic, cutting-edge, practical, surreal, sinister even? Is this appropriate to your target consumer group? Will this make it stand out from the competition?

3. Think about the biggest TV and cinema successes of the last year or so. Might any of them, either in style or content, lend themselves to your campaign?

4. Do the same for technological trends.

5. Are there any well-known people who might serve as the 'face' of your product? Would they be used reverentially or ironically?

6. Look at the ideas you have generated so far. Could you imagine them lasting beyond one campaign? Why? How do they relate to what you might call the zeitgeist? Can you see how they might be adapted to future trends?

PRINCIPLE 6:
THE MEDIUM IS – OR AT LEAST HAS A SERIOUS IMPACT ON – THE MESSAGE

1. Campaigns are increasingly multimedia. How would a poster treatment of your creative concept differ from a press version?

2. What might a cinema or TV spot add to your campaign?

3. What kinds of guerrilla and non-traditional advertising might be used to reach your target audience more effectively?

4. Think of an idea for a viral ad. What would make people want to share this with one another? Would it also make them want to buy your product?

5. How might you use email or other forms of contemporary communications to create an extra bond with customers? The internet is in its infancy: don't assume that all the best ideas have already been thought of.

PRINCIPLE 7:
THERE'S NO SUCH THING AS BAD PUBLICITY

1. Is there a way that your campaign could be extended or remoulded in order to invite (free) press coverage? Why might newspapers/broadcasters be interested in it?

2. Plan a press release and VNR (video news release) to highlight the 'news' aspects of your campaign.

3. Is your advert designed to provoke a strong reaction in viewers? If so, will it put off your target consumers?

4. Could a 'shockvertising' approach usefully be adopted for your campaign?

PRINCIPLE 8:
RESTRICTIONS WILL SET YOU FREE

1. Make sure your ad makes no claims that are untrue or misleading.

2. If your campaign is intended for more than one market (and, thanks to the internet, campaigns are increasingly global in their reach), might it be interpreted differently in different cultural contexts? If so, does the campaign need to be altered to prevent such misunderstandings?

3. Restrictions can be turned to your advantage. Are there things that, for whatever reason, you're not allowed to mention directly but that might be alluded to in some more tangential way? Across history, censorship has often proved a great creative force.

PRINCIPLE 9: ONCE IS NEVER ENOUGH

PRINCIPLE 10: IGNORE ALL RULES AND PRESCRIPTIONS

1. Where is your ad going to appear? How can you ensure that it achieves maximum impact in terms of its placement on the page, etc? If it's for television, make sure it's shown around programmes that appeal to your target audience.

2. Make a costing of your campaign. How much will it cost to make the ad in the first place? How much will it then cost to buy space in magazines/on billboards to make sure people actually see it?

1. No rules or prescriptions will ever ensure that an ad is going to be successful. An idea may fulfil all the criteria and pass all the tests listed above and still fail. On the other hand, an idea that fails all of the tests mentioned here is unlikely to succeed. But in the end advertising is a matter of instinct. Be logical in your approach but don't forget to be bold too!

INDEX

PICTURE CREDITS

Every effort has been made to give credit to the appropriate source, if there are any omissions or errors please contact us and we will undertake to make any corrections in the next printing.

The following images are courtesy of **The Advertising Archives**: BMW, 2004 UK p 8t; Conservative Party, 1979, UK p 8b; California Dept of Health Service, 2000s, USA p 10; French Connection, 2000s, UK p 12; Volkswagen, 1990s, UK p 15; Guinness, 1930s, UK p 16; Land Rover, 2010, UK p 19; Haagen-Dazs, 1990s, UK p 20; Smint, 2000s, UK p 23; Tango, 2009, UK p 24; Pepsi, 1970s, UK p 25; Haagen-Dazs, 1990s, p 26t; Howard Johnsons, 1951, USA p 26b; Ben & Jerrys, 2006, UK p 26b; Ben & Jerrys, 2010, UK p 27; Dulux Paint, 1990s, UK p 28; Financial Times, 2007, UK p 33; Rolls-Royce, 1958, USA p 34; French Tourism, 1960s, USA p 35; Nike, 2010, UK p 36; Ronseal, 2000s, UK p 37; Remington, 1979, UK p 39; Strand, 1959, UK p 40; Ferrero Rocher, 1993, UK p 41; Gillette, 1905, UK p 45; Volkswagen Beetle, 1961, UK p 46; Boddingtons, 1990s, UK p 47; Bovril, 1930s, UK p 48; Heinz, 2007, UK p 49; Evian, 2011, UK p 50m; Ribena, 2010, UK p 50b; Heinz, 1970s, UK p 51t; Smash, 1974, UK p 51b; Mars, 2009, UK p 52t; Milk Board, 1958, UK 52b; Wendy's, 1984, USA p 53; Sony, 1995, UK p 54t; Sony Bravia, 2005, UK p 54b; Maxell, 1980s, UK p 55; Coca-cola, 1942, USA p 58t; Coca-cola, 1930s, Italy p 58b; Fedex, 2010, Brazil p 60; BMW, 1990s, UK p 61t; Lego, 1970s, p UK 61m; HIV, 2000s, USA p 61b; Aga, 2000s, UK p 62t; Sunday Times, 2011, UK p 62b; Virgin Atlantic, 2000s, UK p 63t; Heineken, 1980s, UK p 63m; Apple Macbook, 2008, UK p 63b; Dubonnet, 1930s, France p 64t; Christian Dior, 1970s, UK p 64b; Fougasse, 1940s, UK 64b; Jules Cheret, 1900s, France p 65; Saul Bass, 1959, USA p 65t; Abram Games, 1940s, UK p 65b; Samusocial, 2010, France p 66; Volkswagen, 2011, China p 67; World Wildlife Fund, 2008, UK p 68; French Connection, 2010, UK p 69; Selfridges, 2009, UK p 69t; Project Ocean, 2011, UK p 70; Dixons, 2009, UK p 72; Diesel, 2010, UK p 73b; Harvey Nichols, 2000s, UK p 73t; Modess, 1952, USA p 73t; National Lottery, 2010, UK p 74t; Trojan, 2008, UK p 74t; Kirin, 1990s, UK p 75; Mars, 2000s, UK p 76; T-mobile, 2011, Netherlands p 77t; Lord Kitchener, 1914, UK p 77b; ACLU, 2007, USA p 80; Unilever, 2009, USA p 81; TImex, 1940s, USA p 82; Hamlet cigars, 1987, UK p 83; Bufferin, 1950s, USA p 84; Men's Dry Control Hairspray, 1971, UK p 85; Club 18-30, 1996, UK p 86; Aids Condoms poster, 1990s, Australia, p 86; Stop the War Coalition, 2004, UK p 87t; Sketchly, 1990s, UK p 87t; Labour Party, 2005, UK p 87b; Ryanair, 2000s, France p 87b; Guerrilla Girls, 1980s, USA p 88t; Comparethemarket.com, 2011, UK p 88b; Andrex, 2010, UK p 89; Bird's Eye, 1974, UK p 90; After Eights, 1970s, UK p 91; Heineken, 2004, UK p 92t; HM Revenue & Customs, 2007, UK p 92b; Recruitment poster, 1915, UK p 93; Holsten Pils, 1983, UK p 94; PG Tips, 1970, UK p 95;

Cadbury's, 1970s, UK p 95b; Carling Black Label, 1989, UK p 96t; Volkswagen, 2005, UK p 96b; Walker's crisps, 2010, UK p 98; Nescafe, 2001, UK p 99t; Brut 33, 1970s, UK 99m; Electricity Association, 1990s, UK p 99b; Esso, 1960s, USA p 100; Oxo, 1950s, UK p 102; Hathaway Shirts, 1960s, USA p 103; Maidenform, 1960s, USA p 104; Revlon, 1988, USA p 105; Volkswagen Golf, 1988, UK p 105; British Airways, 2005, UK p 106; Health Education Authority, 1970s, UK p 106; Rolex, 2005, UK p 107; Cadbury's Flake, 2006, UK p 108; Dove, 2004, UK p 108b; Tom Ford, 2010, UK p 109b; Wall's Magnum, 2000s, France p 109t; Maltesers, 2000s, UK p 110; Apple iPod, 2004, UK p 111; Visa, 2000s, UK p 111b; Courage Best Beer, 1979, UK p 112; British Rail, 1988, UK p 112; Hovis, 1970s, UK p 113; Economist, 2010, 2011, UK p 117; Ariel, 2003, India p 121t; Araldite, 1990s, UK p 121b; Planet M, 2001, India p 123; Jobs in Town, 2008, Germany p 128; Gumtree, 2010, UK p 132; Whiskas, 2000s, UK p 137; Gossard Wonderbra, 1994, UK p 139; United Colors of Benetton, 2011, UK p 140; Benetton, 1996, UK p 141; Sanitol, 2010, India p 142; Deutscher Tierschutzbund, 2010, Germany p 143; UNICEF, 2003, UK p 144; Central Office of Information, 1989, UK p 145t; NHS, 2006, UK p 145b; Guinness, 1996, UK p 140; Double Diamond, 1950s, UK p 150; Heineken, 1970s, UK p 152; Benson & Hedges, 1980s, 1977, UK p 153; Apple Computers Mackintosh, 1984, UK p 156; KitKat, 1960s, UK p 158; KitKat, 2000s, UK p 159; Absolut Vodka, 1980, USA p 163; Economist, 2002, UK p 164; Smirnoff, 1999, UK p 165.

Other sources: Courtesy MRM Meteorite Agency, Costa coffee p 84b and Argos, 2007, p 130; Courtesy Mizkan, 2008, Japan p 50; Courtesy Ajinomoto, 2006, Japan p 69b; Courtesy The Jupiter Drawing Room, 2009, South Africa p 71; Courtesy of Masterfoods, 2000s, Italy p 74b; Courtesy Clarity Coverdale Fury (art director: Jim Landry; copywriter: Michael Atkinson; creative director: Jac Coverdale; production: Caroline Gibbs), 2003, USA p 118; Courtesy HBO Television Network p 122; Courtesy DDB, Canada p 124; Courtesy Grey Agency, Argentina, p 124; Courtesy Haxan Films p 127;

ACKNOWLEDGEMENTS

The author would like to express his gratitude to all of the advertising professionals and commentators who have helped him to understand how their world works, in particular Dan Douglass, Jan Pester and Mike Widdis.